SATISFYING OUR INNATE DESIRE
[TO KNOW GOD]

Satisfying Our Innate Desire

[to Know God]

*How We Can Be Spiritually
Awake and Live As the Divine
Beings We Really Are*

ROY EUGENE DAVIS

CSA PRESS
The Publishing Department of Center for Spiritual Awareness
Lakemont, Georgia (U.S.A.)

ISBN 0-87707-290-6

CSA Press
Post Office Box 7
Lakemont, Georgia 30552-0001

Telephone (706) 782-4723
Fax (706) 782-4560
e-mail csainc@csa-davis.org
Web Site www.csa-davis.org

CSA Press is the publishing department
of Center for Spiritual Awareness,
with office and retreat center at
151 CSA Lane, Lakemont, Georgia.

PRINTED IN THE UNITED STATES OF AMERICA

Let us reverently acknowledge
the reality of God in and around us;
the enlightened sages of all traditions;
the divine nature of every person;
and the essence of our own being,
knowing that here we are one with
Infinite Consciousness and that all
knowledge of it and it's processes
is within us.

Foreword

Every man, woman, and child should be informed that an enlivening Power is nourishing our universe and they can learn to cooperate with it. When they do, their lives will be enhanced, their worthy endeavors will be successful, and they will experience rapid, progressive spiritual growth that will ultimately, in the course of time, completely satisfy the desire of their heart.

During my early teenage years, in a rural area of northern Ohio, I began to earnestly inquire about the reality of God. Although I had always been aware of a "benevolent Presence" that I could not then accurately define, I knew it was in and around me, as it was in and around everyone and everything. I read the writings of Ralph Waldo Emerson and several books on religion, psychology, and yoga, and prayed fervently for a more vivid awareness of the presence of God.

In early spring of 1949, I avidly read Paramahansa Yogananda's book *Autobiography of a Yogi*, and in late December traveled to Los Angeles, California, to meet him, and under his guidance began a four-year period of intensive spiritual practice.

Since then, I have never wavered in my resolve to know God. I can affirm, from personal experience, that fervent aspiration, dedicated resolve, persistent right endeavors, and God's grace will enable a sincere truth seeker to experience spiritual growth that will culminate in Self-discovery and God-realization.

What I have learned is described in the following pages in the hope that this information will be of value to the reader who aspires to know God.

Roy Eugene Davis

Spring, 2003
Lakemont, Georgia (U.S.A.)

PUBLISHER'S NOTE

For optimum benefits, read this book several times. When a word or concept is not understood, refer to the glossary.

CONTENTS

CHAPTER ONE

Why We Want to Know God

To get at the core of God ... one must first get into the core of the self ... Go to the depths of the soul ... the secret place of the Most High, to the roots, to the heights, for all that God can do is focused there. – *Meister Eckhart (1260 – 1327)*

A compelling urge from the deepest level of our being makes us yearn to have our awareness restored to its original, pure state and we cannot be completely satisfied until this is permanently accomplished.

When thoughts and emotions are calm, we can intuitively discern that we are not mere physical creatures fated to be forever confined by illusions or limited by conditions over which we are powerless to control. We may then be aware that we are immortal, spiritual beings with innate powers yet to be actualized and an inherent capacity to be fully awake to the truth of what we are and our relationship with the Infinite.

When you have such insights, be happy, for you can then be inspired and motivated to decisively choose to rise above habitual ways of thinking, feeling, and behaving which may not always be compatible with your aspiration to be Self- and God-realized.

God is not what most people think God to be. Mental

concepts fall short of defining what God is. It is human nature to imagine God to be a cosmic person: male, female, or androgynous (having both characteristics). Or to presume God to be kind, capable of rewarding good behavior, punishing bad behavior, healing painful conditions, and saving souls from the suffering and limitations common to ordinary human conditions. God may be imagined as a supreme intelligence, a cosmic mind, an omniscient, omnipotent, formless being, or as goodness or love in accord with one's ideas regarding the meanings of those concepts.

Millions of people regularly pray to God even if their prayers are not answered because they feel that they should, hope that a response will eventually be forthcoming, feel better when they do it, or have no place else to turn for help or solace. And millions of people faithfully participate in private or public ritual worship without having a vivid or meaningful sense of relationship with God.

Although the innate urge to know God is present in everyone, few people know how to actually experience the reality of God. Every soul, as an individualized unit of pure consciousness, is living *in* God now. This truth (fact) only has to be acknowledged and realized.

The often asked questions: What is God?, How can I find God?, Why does God allow suffering?, are based on lack of understanding of God as a field of supreme Consciousness of which we are individualized units.

God need not be sought as though existing in a remote place. The invisible Presence is all-pervading; its ruling power is expressing in and as everything in the universe. Because we are units of God's being, all knowledge of God is within us.

God is not responsible for human suffering and misfortune. Unpleasant conditions result from lack of God-knowledge, mental and emotional confusion, and unwise behaviors. By self-training in rational, optimistic thinking and by conforming our behaviors to impersonal laws of cause and effect, most suffering can be avoided and good fortune can be experienced.

Many people who say they want to know God and to live freely and enjoyably are not always sincere. They want only enough knowledge of God and of how to live better that will enable them to have a little more peace of mind and personal circumstances that are somewhat improved. Dedicated truth seekers who choose to learn how to grow to emotional and spiritual maturity can soon rise above ordinary human conditions and awaken rapidly through the stages of spiritual growth.

When we know God as God is, our awareness is no longer ordinary (fragmented and blurred by mental and emotional confusion and subconscious influences); it is illumined (clarified). Knowledge of our true nature in relationship to the wholeness of life then emerges. This ideal state of spiritual enlightenment is not only possible for every sincere person to realize; all are destined to awaken to it. The possibility of doing so exists at every moment.

Various names for God have been, and are, used in an attempt to describe the supreme Reality beyond the boundaries of space, time, and relative conditions.

The word *god* (Old English, "the highest good") comes from Germanic and Indo-European languages in which a corresponding ancestor word was used. In the *Rig-veda*, the oldest known religious scripture, which was first transmitted in the oral tradition, the words *puru-hutas* ("much invoked") are found. To *invoke* is to "call upon or appeal to" for help.

The Israelites used the name *Yahweh*, "the God of our fathers" (Old Testament). When Moses, who was educated in Egypt, asked for knowledge of God, his self-response was, "I am what I am." *Elohim*, a Hebrew name for God, can signify a variety of gods or concepts of God that people might have.

Muslims refer to "the Creator of heaven and earth who alone can redeem souls and provide material sustenance" as *al-Lah*, the one Reality. The aspect of divinity turned toward the world is referred to as "The Face of God." In the *Qur'an* (Koran), the sacred book of the Islamic faith, ninety-nine attributes of God are named, which may be recited to nurture devotion and an awareness of the presence of God.

Zoroastrians (in Persia, circa 600 B.C.E.) referred to God as *Ahura Masda*, "the Wise Creator, Lord or Ruler."

Adherents of Hinduism, more accurately *Sanatana Dharma* (the eternal, righteous way), refer to pure Consciousness, as *Brahman*. The name used for its expansive, expressive aspect is *Brahma*. Many other names are used for a variety of aspects, attributes, and powers which make possible God's manifestations and actions. Some names indicate the gender attributed to gods (cosmic powers) and goddesses (creative forces). Forceful, controlling influences are thought of as masculine. Characteristics related to manifestation and nurturing of the worlds are considered as feminine.

Monotheism (*mono*, one; *theos*, god) is the basic doctrine of Judaism, Christianity, Islam, Hinduism, and some traditional African religions. Within them are subdivisions and sects with teachings emphasized in accord with the philosophical ideas and practices of their adherents.

Some individuals deny the existence of God. Others say that God created the universe, but is removed from it, has no influence on phenomena, and provides no supernatural revelation. These two erroneous opinions (*atheism* and *deism*, respectively) result from lack of accurate knowledge of God or insufficiently developed intellectual or intuitive powers.

We need not be concerned about the diverse opinions or habitual or random behaviors of others who do not share our views or preferences. The paths chosen by truth seekers who endeavor to know God are in accord with their understanding, psychological temperament, and capacity to comprehend. What is of utmost importance for us is that we be committed to discovering what is true and that our insights illumine our minds and enable us to live freely and effectively.

Affirmation

I am firmly resolved to allow my innate
urge to have my awareness fully restored
to wholeness freely express.

Answers to Questions About
Why We Want to Know God

If our innate urge is to know God, why is it that we are not always aware of it?

We may not be aware of this inclination because of excessive concern with ordinary, everyday circumstances or because of an egocentric state of awareness which inclines us think, feel, and behave as though we were mortal, physical creatures. Even when we are not conscious of wanting (and needing) to know God, our innate urge to have our awareness restored to its original, pure state of wholeness will, in time, become so compelling that it cannot be ignored.

Now that I am aware of my soul-urge to know God, what can I do to acquire higher understanding that will definitely result in real spiritual growth?

The orderly emergence of innate knowledge of our true nature and the reality of God spontaneously occurs when we allow it to do so. 1) Acquire accurate information about higher realities and what you can do to live effectively. 2) Cultivate an optimistic mental attitude, adhere to a wholesome lifestyle, and aspire to realize the ultimate purpose of your life. 3) Meditate daily until you are established in conscious awareness of your true nature in relationship with the Infinite.

Can anyone who aspires to know God do it?

Any person who fervently aspires to know God can do so because everyone is, at the core of their being, a flawless unit of God. Our spiritual growth, whether slow, faster, or rapid, is determined by the intensity of our aspiration and our effective endeavors that enable us to remove or rise above the obstacles that obscure our perceptions of what is true.

Lack of interest in spiritual growth and intellectual laziness are common characteristics of people who are not inclined to aspire to know God.

Although I sincerely want to know God, I tend to think and feel that God is unreachable and unknowable. What can I do to overcome these thoughts and feelings?

Improve your understanding of your relationship with God. Memorize and frequently remind yourself of this fact:

Nothing separates us from God. It is only the habit of identifying with mental, emotional, and physical states, and with objective phenomena, that causes and sustains the illusion (misperception) of independent existence. When this error in perception is corrected, our awareness is immediately restored to wholeness.

CHAPTER TWO

How to Know What to Believe

I keep six honest serving men
(They taught me everything I knew);
Their names are What and Why and When
And How and Where and Who.
— *Rudyard Kipling (1865 – 1935)*
Just-So Stories (1902) / The Elephant's Child

A *belief* is an act, condition, or habit of having trust or confidence in a person, thing, or idea; conviction in the actuality of something, especially the opinions or doctrines accepted by a group of persons.

Knowledge can be acquired by direct perception, deductive reasoning; inference; and by being informed by someone who is already knowledgeable. Erroneous concepts and beliefs interfere with rational thinking and impair our ability to function effectively. Illusions (flawed perceptions of concepts or of what is observed) cloud our awareness and obscure our perception of what is true. One whose mind and awareness is thus blurred may be inclined to presume that material realities alone exist and that the physical body is one's real identity. By replacing ignorance of the facts with accurate knowledge, it is possible to live an ordinary life skillfully. A truth seeker will not be happy with an ordinary life; only spiritual awakening and unfoldment and actualization of soul qualities will be acceptable.

Newly acquired, valid knowledge comforts the mind and may also confirm our intuitive insights. When newly acquired knowledge is in conflict with what was formerly thought to be true, mild confusion and some symptoms of stress may temporarily result. We may resist and not want to believe it because to do so may require us to change some of our habits of thinking and behavior, lifestyle routines, or relationships.

Spiritual Enlightenment

To be *enlightened* about something is to "know" about it. One who is *spiritually enlightened* knows the true Self— their essence of being—as a unit of the one Reality that emanates and sustains the universe.

Spiritual enlightenment should not be thought of as a condition to be attained in the distant future; it should be acknowledged as our natural state to be experienced at any moment. In some traditions, Self-realization is said to occur in progressive stages, with partial insights preceding more complete discoveries. In other traditions, enlightenment is said to occur as complete realization with preliminary, partial insights (mingled with illusions) providing glimpses of what is yet to be realized.

Early states of identification of awareness with a meditation object are stages of knowing. A meditative sense of oneness with light, sound, bliss, or any other perceived object is defined as "oneness with support" of the perceived object—which should be transcended if oneness without support of an object of perception is to be realized.

So long as a sense of oneness is supported by an object of perception, there is dependency rather than freedom. We may have a sense of identification with the perceived object without having full knowledge of it. Without full knowledge, flawless enlightenment has not yet been realized: the truth seeker is encouraged to persist in right endeavors.

Right endeavors allow beneficial results to be actualized. The recommended right endeavors include rational thinking; cultivation of emotional maturity; a wholesome, disciplined lifestyle; resisting and overcoming harmful inclinations; the performance of constructive actions; and skillful meditation practice.

Meditation practice that only produces a pleasant mood or a sense of communion with a larger Reality, while providing some mental and emotional peace and soul refreshment, does not result in authentic spiritual enlightenment. Some truth seekers struggle for many years in a vain endeavor to become spiritually enlightened, not knowing that, when conditions that blur and confine their awareness are removed, their true nature will be immediately revealed.

Rightly applied spiritual practices purify the mind, clarify awareness, greatly improve intellectual powers, and allow spiritual awakening to occur quickly. For one who aspires to be spiritually enlightened, the first constructive action to perform is to firmly resolve to acquire valid knowledge about the facts of life, how to live effectively, and how to nurture and cooperate with the innate soul-urge to be fully awake.

Karma: Influences That Cause Effects

The word *karma*, derived from Sanskrit *kr*, "to do," is used to describe actions that produce corresponding effects or have the potential to do so. Karmic effects may be immediate or may require time and/or favorable circumstances to allow them to occur. Thoughts, emotional states, aspirations, whims, desires, behaviors, and conscious or unconscious reactions to events can influence our powers of perception and determine our experiences and circumstances.

Relationships between physical actions and their effects are usually obvious. Relationships between mental, emotional, subconscious and unconscious states and our experiences are not always so obvious. We may have forgotten past incidents of trauma or those occasions when memories of fear, frustration, desires, choices, or opinions of others were impressed in the subconscious mind.

When deeply seated mental impressions influence our thoughts, feelings, or behaviors, we may wonder why efforts to think constructively and perform right actions do not always produce the results we desire to have. We may think that our karma is "bad" and wonder what might be done to overcome or banish it. When constructive mental impressions are more influential, we may be thankful because of our "good karma." We may hear someone say, "What I thought and did in the past created bad karma that will probably catch up with me sooner or later." Or,

"I'm doing my best to think positive and perform right actions because I want to accumulate only good karma."

The three classes of karma are:

1. Dormant mental impressions accumulated in the distant or recent past which may or may not be influential in the near or distant future.
2. Mental impressions influential now. If they are positive and supportive, their effects can be allowed. If their influences interfere with thinking and behavior, they can be resisted and neutralized by constructive thinking and actions and by regular meditation that allows superconscious influences to prevail during and after practice. Superconscious states, which are superior to all other states of consciousness, gradually weaken and dissolve the seeds (latent impressions) of karma.
3. Memories now being impressed in the subconscious mind by intentional and random thoughts, feelings, actions, and emotional reactions. All perceptions create impressions in the mind. Knowing this, we should perceive with accuracy and wisely choose our mental and emotional states and our actions.

Although resisting harmful karmic influences and allowing only constructive karma to be accumulated is useful, the ultimate, functional level is to live spontaneously with no karmic influences prevailing. At this stage of spiritual enlightenment, when karmic influences have been neutralized or transcended, we are liberated from the conditions that formerly confined our awareness.

When we choose to live in the right way and engage in constructive actions, much of the potential effects of karma are avoided and we can be more receptive to the actions of grace. Mental and spiritual attunement with others who are spiritually enlightened purifies our mind and awakens our soul forces. Knowledge that is acquired and wisely applied weakens subconscious influences, empowers our will to modify behaviors, and allows spiritual growth to occur more rapidly.

Do not think, feel, or say that you are a helpless victim of past experiences, astrological influences, or environmental conditions. Established in Self-knowledge, make wise choices and think, feel, and act constructively. Anticipate and be receptive to the unplanned good fortune that life can and will provide for you.

Reincarnation

To be embodied is to incarnate. To be embodied again is to reincarnate. Most people who consider physical rebirth to be possible do not have reliable memories of having been on earth prior to their present incarnation. While they may have opinions about reincarnation or "feel" that they have been on earth before, the subject remains a mystery: something not fully understood.

Attempts to prove reincarnation by using hypnosis to remember "past lives" do not produce results which can be verified and can result in fantasy. Perhaps the most reliable "evidence" on which to support a belief in reincarnation is that many spiritually enlightened people say that it occurs.

The usual concept of reincarnation is that souls are attracted to environmental conditions that can provide them opportunities to have their needs satisfied and their desires or aspirations fulfilled. Just as our habitual mental states and states of awareness incline us to have experiences or attract circumstances which correspond to them, so the mental states and states of awareness of souls abiding in subtle realms determine their experiences and circumstances and whether or not they will incarnate again.

A belief in reincarnation is based on a conviction that the soul is independent of the mind and physical body, and may, as is necessary or desired, relate to and express through a mind and physical body, both of which are forms of matter.

The sages of ancient India carefully analyzed the subjects they examined and precisely defined the words they used to describe their observations. The Sanskrit word *atman* is used to refer to a unit of pure consciousness (the true Self). *Jiva* (what we refer to as a soul) is used when referring to a unit of pure consciousness identified with a mind and a realm of matter at a causal, astral, or physical level. The Self is whole, serene, and knowledgeable. When it is not established in Self-awareness and its attention is distracted by, or attracted to, external conditions, it tends to identify with those conditions and temporarily forget its essence. The urge to have its awareness restored to its original wholeness inclines it to awaken to that conscious, free state. That is why, regardless of how confused we are or how complicated our life may be, the desire to awaken to Self- and God-realization eventually becomes compelling.

As we progress through the stages of spiritual awakening, our thoughts become rational, intellect is refined, and powers of intuition improve. Soul forces which were dormant when our awareness was confined by an illusional sense of selfhood (ego) become increasingly influential and refine the nervous system and brain through which our awareness expresses. Nurturing spiritual growth replaces complacency and dispassionate objectivity replaces sentimental thinking and behavior.

In some ancestor-oriented societies, whose main concern is the maintenance and enhancement of the continuity and prosperity of the kinship group, it is believed that children are reincarnations of specific ancestors. When it is determined who the returned ancestor is believed to be, the child is given the name of that person.

Among some people in Europe and America who may not have had a systematic religious foundation, reincarnation is often viewed as a random occurrence with no organized philosophy to explain it. In most parts of the world people have, at one time or another, attempted to contact departed souls to prove the continuity of life after physical death.

In America and England, until late in the last century a movement known as spiritualism was promoted by "mediums" who, it was claimed, could communicate with departed souls. In our current era mediums have, for the most part, been replaced by "channelers" and "clairvoyants" who perform in a similar way and whose "messages" are unreliable and their behaviors fraudulent. Individuals who claim to regularly talk with or communicate messages from departed souls are either deluded, prone to fantasy, or are knowingly pretending to do it. Truth seekers are advised to avoid such activities.

Shortly before Paramahansa Yogananda left his body, he told some disciples that, after his departure, many individuals would claim to be in communication with him. He said that he would not communicate in this way. Yet, within a few months after his transition, several spiritualist mediums claimed to be receiving messages from him.

Evaluating Sacred Scriptures

Sacred scriptures are writings which are usually concerned with 1) the expression and transmission of spoken and written sounds or words as vehicles of holy or sacred power; 2) the meaning, values, ideals, and self-identity of a group of people and recommended standards of normal and ideal behaviors; 3) directing believers to a transcendental reality; 4) defining and resolving human problems or concerns; 5) explaining and emphasizing ways that will enable the actualization of divine qualities.

Writings composed by people who are considered (by their believers) to have been inspired need to be thoughtfully read and their meanings discerned. None can be declared as inerrant (free from flaws). The individuals who composed or collected them were not all spiritually enlightened; some of the information was directed to people of a particular time and culture; and translations and interpretations through the years may have partially, or completely, changed some of the original concepts and teachings. Acquiring insight into any scripture requires use of our powers of reason, discriminative intelligence, and intuition.

A central theme in most sacred scriptures is that salvation (soul freedom) is possible and is emphasized as the ultimate aim of life to be accomplished while one is still incarnated rather than as a possible future event to occur during or after leaving the physical body. The means by which salvation may be experienced are variously described. The core teaching is that we should be honest and compassionate and engage in spiritual practices such as contemplative prayer and meditation. We can then gradually awaken from ordinary states of mind and awareness to higher states, Self-realization, cosmic consciousness, and God-realization in the present incarnation.

Merely hoping to enjoy a heaven-like existence as a reward for moral or "good" behavior, blind belief in a religious doctrine, the performance of charitable works, or expecting a savior-god to redeem us will not ensure our spiritual enlightenment and soul freedom. The only way to experience soul liberation is to do what is necessary to allow it to be realized. Right thinking and right living supported by effective spiritual practice removes all mental and physical obstacles to spiritual growth.

The spiritual path is enjoyable and progressive for sincere truth seekers who are emotionally mature and responsible for their thoughts and actions. It is usually difficult and slow for persons who are emotionally immature or complacently satisfied to live an ordinary self-centered existence. In the latter instance, there is a possibility that a life-changing event or unexpected conversion episode may occur that will result in a spontaneous, beneficial transformation of awareness.

Everyone will have their awareness restored to wholeness. If past experiences are then remembered, they will be known for what they were: mere incidents that only seemed to be significant when one was but "dreaming" because asleep to the truth.

A precise definition of a subject or of a procedure to be used is helpful in endeavors to comprehend it. When a mental concept is not precise, thinking will not be reasonable, conclusions will be faulty, and attempts to communicate it to others will result in misunderstanding.

It is common to hear someone refer to God as a higher or larger self or as mind or love—words that do not accurately communicate the reality of God. Some people err by thinking of the soul as the subconscious mind, or the essence of God in them rather than what it is—their real nature. Every soul is a pure-conscious unit of God.

I have heard people say, "It doesn't matter what words are used so long as the understanding we have allows us to have the results we want." Translation: "I just want enough understanding to satisfy my mind and enable me to accomplish my self-centered purposes."

When a process to be used is not comprehended, its application may not produce the desired results. If we try to pray or meditate without knowing how to do it effectively, we are not likely to be satisfied with the outcome. When planning to achieve goals by using creative imagination and physical actions, if our knowledge of how to proceed is flawed, results will be unpredictable.

How to Pray Effectively

Intention and devotion help to make prayers effective. Intention determines the form of prayer. One may pray to express gratitude, ask for help, endeavor to intercede on behalf of others, or have a conscious awareness of the presence of God that culminates in a sense of communion—a sense of intimate, gratifying relationship with God. Devotion enables us to concentrate on and merge our awareness with that to which our attention is directed.

- Prayer as an expression of gratitude for good fortune that we already have or know to be forthcoming, is a way to acknowledge the Source that provides for us. Being thankful for our good fortune enables us to be aware of and receptive to a continuous flow of supportive resources and events. The saying, "Be thankful for your blessings," is good advice.

- Asking (petitioning) God for what is desired or needed attracts a response from omnipresent Consciousness. The key to effective asking is to believe that what is wanted or needed is already present and available. Belief attracts supportive events as well as causes them to occur. When you prayerfully ask for your desires or needs to be satisfied, keep it simple. God already knows what you want or need; prayerful asking enables you to clarify your thinking and be receptive.

If you cannot clearly define your wants or needs, ask

for—and expect—your "highest good" to be actualized. Continue until you have a vivid, intuitive awareness and feeling that you have what you requested. Desires may not always be instantly fulfilled, needs may not always be immediately provided for, healing may not always be sudden. While results can be quick, it is possible that outer events need to first emerge to make possible the ideal circumstances you want or need. Have faith: *believe* and *feel* the reality of the results you desire to have.

- When compassionately led to intercede on behalf of others: meditate until you are God-centered; think of those for whose welfare you are praying; include them in your awareness of God; and wish for their highest good. Sit quietly until you feel, at the core of your being, that all is well. You may also pray like this for improvement of social and environmental circumstances. Avoid anxiety about the outcome.

- When praying for a sense of communion with God: pray aloud to declare your intention; pray quietly; whisper your prayer; pray mentally until words cease; then abide in the silence, fervently yearning to have your heart's desire fulfilled. Persist until a shift of awareness and viewpoint occurs that results in vivid awareness of God. Rest there for a while.

Contemplative Meditation Practice

Meditation is inward attention directed to an object on which one chooses to concentrate, with aspiration to know about or identify with it.

Many people practice meditation for the relaxation, stress reduction, and mind-calming benefits which enable them to live more effectively. Some medical clinics provide meditation classes for patients who need to manage stress or are recovering from an illness. For all who are intent on Self- and God-realization, meditation is an effective way to elicit superconscious states and clarify awareness. When the mind is calm and awareness is clear, the essence of being can be experienced.

Studies conducted at Penn State University, during which the brains of subjects were scanned when they were settled in a peaceful meditative state, revealed that the front lobes of the brain were usually involved. The front region is related to creativity, discernment, and choice-making. It was also noted that when centers in the upper, back area of both hemispheres of the brain (which process sensory perceptions and enable us to relate to space, time, and our environment) were quiet, meditators later said they experienced a sense of unbounded, timeless awareness. Stimulation of the left temporal region of the brain with a mild magnetic field caused some subjects to report a sense of a "presence" in the room. In another study, when a brain center above and behind the right ear was stimulated with a mild electric current, subjects sometimes described sensations of being out of the body. It is also known that some people's obsession with religious ideas are related to pressure caused by tumors in specific areas of the brain or other abnormal brain activities.

When the mind and brain are deprived of sensory input, a variety of unusual subjective perceptions may be experienced. Many reported instances of "mystical experiences" and "revelations" are mind- and/or brain-produced rather than the results of superconscious states. Superconscious states enhance our awareness, elicit our innate knowledge, and improve our intellectual powers.

Meditators on an enlightenment path are advised to avoid preoccupation with subjective phenomena. What is seen or sensed during meditation should be "gone beyond" in order to know and experience our changeless nature.

Intuition: The Faculty of Direct Perception

Intuition is the capacity to directly perceive. Almost everyone has had an experience of "just knowing" something without any objective circumstances being present. Intuitive powers can and should be cultivated. Use intuition with rational thinking when making plans, solving problems, and endeavoring to understand a situation. Use it when interacting with others, during metaphysical study, when praying for guidance, or meditating.

Because intuitive powers are innate to the soul, when cultivating them, avoid excessive effort. Consider intuition to be a natural capacity, rather than an ability to be acquired. Intuitive powers are often functional at an early age, then may become weaker as children and young adults assume the mental attitudes and behaviors of their friends and others whose awareness is ordinary while endeavoring to adapt to their environmental circumstances. Intuition is accurate knowing, although an emotional surge or feeling of certainty may also be present.

The Path of Spiritual Discipleship

A *disciple* is a "student" who is intent on learning. A disciple on a spiritual path should be fully committed to learning and to applying what is learned. Some individuals who consider themselves to be disciples are not as committed as they should (and could) be. Their mental states are superficial and their behaviors are often determined by whims rather than by conscious intention. My guru asked disciples to be "one hundred percent" devoted to their spiritual path. Not all of them were thus committed. Those who were, experienced rapid progress.

Some spiritual aspirants are reluctant to make a commitment to discipleship because they are afraid that they may have to change some of their mental attitudes and behaviors—which they will, if they are to be successful in their endeavors. Learning what not to do is just as important as learning what must be done, and doing it. The purpose of spiritual discipleship is not merely to be able to enjoy an improved human condition, it is to rapidly awaken to God-realization and liberation of consciousness.

Affirmation

I use my powers of discriminative
intelligence and intuition to discern what is true
and live in accord with that knowledge.

How to Use a Personal Prayer Journal

When you pray to have your needs met or a desire fulfilled, write what you have asked for in a notebook or personal journal. Write "fulfilled" beside the entry when your prayer is answered.

Date: _____
Prayer Request for:
Guidance in regard to _____.

Date: _____
Healing of (the condition) _____.

Date: _____
Healing for (person's name) _____.

Date: _____
Healing for the highest good of (person's name(s) or social or environmental condition.

_____

_____

_____

_____

Date:_____
Prosperity

Date: _____
Solution to a problem _____.

Date: _____
Satisfying meditation practice.

Date: _____
Self-knowledge.

Date: _____
Awareness of the presence of God.

Write any other needs or desires.

_____

_____

_____

_____

_____

_____

_____

_____

What you pray for, *believe* that you have it.
Be thankful.

How to Practice Meditation

If you are a novice meditator, this procedure will enable you meditate effectively. If you are a regular meditator, your practice will be improved.

When possible, meditate in a quiet place at the same time every day. You will then be more likely to eagerly anticipate your practice session, which will be enjoyable and productive.

1. Sit upright in a comfortable chair. A seated cross-legged posture is also suitable, if it is comfortable.

2. Close your eyes. Put your attention in the front and higher regions of the brain. Inhale deeply, exhale and relax.

3. Pause for a few moments to acknowledge that you are a spiritual being abiding *in* God. If you want to silently pray for attunement with the Infinite and an awareness of God's presence, do so.

4. If meditation occurs spontaneously, let it flow. If meditation does not occur spontaneously, use a technique to elicit relaxation and calm the mind. When you are relaxed and peaceful, disregard the meditation technique. Be alert and attentive as you patiently watch and wait with your awareness focused in the front and higher brain.

5. Sit for as long as you are inclined, until you are peaceful and any resistance to sitting is absent.

Conclude the practice session. Open your eyes, sit for a moment to adapt to your environment, and resume your normal activities.

Note: Before concluding your practice session, it can be helpful to:

1. Pray for the welfare and spiritual fulfillment of everyone, everywhere.
2. Know and feel your oneness with the wholeness of life and remind yourself that, as you think and act constructively, you always have the full support of the universe. The resources and supportive events, circumstances, and relationships that are needed for your highest good, will spontaneously emerge in divine order (appropriately and harmoniously). Be thankful for this assurance.

This simple procedure can be used by anyone for the purpose of experiencing deep relaxation, mental calmness, and clarity of awareness. Allow twenty minutes to accomplish a relaxed, calm state and sit for a while in the deep silence.

Sit longer if you choose to do so, to enjoy the deep silence or to contemplate a chosen object or theme.

Answers to Questions About
How to Know What to Believe

Does spiritual enlightenment always occur as a sudden revelation, or does it gradually emerge over a period of time? What can be done to quicken the process?

It can occur suddenly or it may emerge gradually. To more quickly awaken to Self- and God-realization, adhere to a regimen of wholesome living and attend to spiritual practices. *Complete* spiritual practice includes disciplined thinking and behavior, astute (insightful) examination of our true nature and of higher realities, and surrender to God. Effective spiritual practice soon removes obstacles to Self-realization.

To "surrender to God" is to discern the difference between our true essence of being and our illusional sense of selfhood (ego), and transcend it.

Can Self- and God-realization be had without having to engage in intensive spiritual practices?

Our true nature and the full reality of God can be immediately realized when the mind is calm and our awareness is clear. The two primary obstacles to Self-realization are mental restlessness and the mistaken belief that we are other than pure-conscious beings.

Even when the mind is calm, an illusional sense of

selfhood may persist. When the illusional sense of selfhood is dissolved, pure consciousness remains.

Right spiritual practice calms the mind, restrains subliminal drives which cause mental restlessness and emotional unrest, and allows innate knowledge to emerge. "Right" spiritual practices are those which are effective. Practices which are believed to be effective, but are not, are useless.

When you are meditating and the mind is calm, gently inquire, with intention rather than words, "What is the truth about what I am in relationship to God." Sit quietly, inclined to know. Watch and wait. Sooner or later you will experience an adjustment of viewpoint that will enable you to clearly know what you are and what God is. If realization does not immediately occur, be patient. Daily sit in the silence, wanting to know, and you will eventually awaken to what is true.

It is a waste of time, energy, and personal resources to frantically seek outside of yourself in an endeavor to learn "new" or "unique" methods, hoping to accomplish authentic spiritual growth. While there are useful practices to learn and apply, when your mind is calm and meditative contemplation flows smoothly, all of the preliminary methods can be disregarded.

You are already *that* which you desire to realize. At the innermost core of your being you are now serene and knowledgeable. Remove or transcend the mental states and illusional beliefs that cloud your awareness and obscure your perception of what you are, and you will be established in Self- and God-realization.

Does gender (male or female) have anything to do with our potential to be spiritually enlightened?

Because we are spiritual beings, everyone has the same potential to awaken to Self- and God-realization.

Why is it that, with approximately six billion human beings on the planet, so few are spiritually enlightened?

In our current era, the awareness of most people is ordinary (blurred and fragmented), as indicated by their mental states and behaviors. Although it is believed that human beings have been on the planet for one million (or more) years, it was only about ten thousand years ago that hunting and gathering of food began to be replaced by food crop cultivation and the organized establishment of more permanent social groups.

Although the trend of human evolution may seem to be slow, it is inexorable: it persists and prevails. We are now in an era of an accelerated emergence of innate soul knowledge that is resulting in scientific, technological, and spiritual discovery, and this trend will continue for several thousand years. The changes that have occurred in the collective consciousness of human beings during the past two hundred years are only a preview of what is yet to happen.

There are probably more spiritually enlightened people among us than we know about.

In regard to karma: why should we have to experience the effects of past thoughts and actions if we are not aware of them now, or if our current thoughts and actions are wisely chosen and constructive?

Until we are spiritually conscious, we may not be aware of mental impressions in the subconscious level of the mind which influence our thoughts, feelings, and behaviors. Constructive thoughts, feelings, and actions resist, weaken, and neutralize harmful subconscious influences. The more spiritually aware we are, the less we are influenced by karmic conditions or by events that occur in our environment.

What determines where and when souls incarnate?

Except in rare instances, souls are unconsciously attracted to an environment that is compatible with their state of awareness and influential karmic tendencies. Some souls may consciously desire to return because they feel that they will be more comfortable here or have unfinished earth-life duties to complete. When a soul chooses to return, its awareness is blurred and it may not remember having made the choice. Some people say they feel that they came here with a purpose but they don't know what it is or how to discover it. The ultimate purpose for our being in this world is to awaken from the "dream of mortality" to realization of our true nature and God. While we are undergoing this process, it is helpful to us, and to others, to render some kind of useful service to others, society, and the planet.

What should our thoughts and feelings be in regard to people we have loved who have left this realm?

Continue to love and bless them without trying to communicate with them. After allowing a reasonable period of time to come to terms with your sense of loss, replace feelings of loss or grief with thoughts and feelings of gratitude for having known them. Release them to their higher good. Whenever you think of them, breathe a silent prayer or wish for their total well-being and spiritual fulfillment.

Why did God express as souls? Why does God allow souls to incarnate into oppressive conditions, be born with defects or impairments, or die at any early age?

God is not a cosmic person who decides to express as units or souls. Souls are individualized when the Oversoul aspect of supreme Consciousness interacts with its emanated power (Om). Because God is not a cosmic person, God can neither allow nor prevent the events and conditions that occur. What occurs in the mundane realms does so in accord with cause and effect. This is not to say that a child born with defects or impairments or who dies at an early age is being punished for past actions or thoughts. It is more likely that because the soul's awareness was blurred, it was possible for it to be attracted to conditions which were unfortunate—just as some conditions which we experience on a daily basis may be the result of our temporary lack of alertness.

Some people say that belief in karma and reincarnation makes possible an understanding of why some people are

*born into oppressive circumstances, while others are pro-
vided with good fortune, and why some people suffer from
disease, accidents, or other painful or debilitating events
while others are healthy and prosperous. Aren't some of
these ideas simplistic or false?*

Yes, they are often simplistic or not true. The experiences of most people are in accord with their prevailing
states of awareness rather than their prior thoughts or
actions. When our awareness is unenlightened, we may
experience conditions or circumstances that people commonly encounter. Incidents of misfortune can be mini-
mized and avoided by cultivating spiritual awareness.

*When we leave this realm, will we see and be reunited with
family members, friends, or other people with whom we
have had a close relationship?*

We may, or may not, see or renew relationships with
our family members, or others we have known, when we
leave the physical body. If there are strong mental, emotional, or spiritual bonds, it is possible if we go to the same
realm. It is not a good idea to look forward to such experiences when we make our transition; it is better to medi-
tatively aspire to be spiritually enlightened, then allow
what happens to occur.

Some individuals who had a near-death experience
later reported having seen and communicated with people
they once knew. Although such perceptions are usually
mind- or brain-produced, there may be some experiences
which are authentic. During a near-death episode, an
adherent of a religious tradition may "see" Jesus, Krishna,

or another saint-like being and talk or intuitively communicate with them. These perceptions are also usually in accord with one's subconscious images or expectations. A positive side-benefit of such experiences is that one who has had them is often inspired and motivated to live more wisely and purposefully.

Is it of value to try to remember past incarnations?

I do not know of any spiritually enlightened person who recommends doing this. If what seems to be a memory of a past incarnation provides useful insight that enables you to live more effectively, it can be of value. Otherwise, it is best to make the most of the knowledge and the opportunities you have now to live up to your highest potential. Preoccupation with past incarnations, real or imagined, is a distraction from matters which are of greater importance to you.

How can returning to the physical realm be avoided?

The certain way to avoid a future incarnation is to nurture your spiritual growth until you are spiritually enlightened and permanently liberated.

If I am God-realized in this incarnation, will I also be God-realized if I have a future incarnation?

If realization is flawless, it will persist. If it is not flawless when departing from this realm, one may continue to awaken in astral or causal realms or experience a temporary return to conditioned states of awareness. For this reason, it is important to be fully Self- and God-realized before leaving the body. No real spiritual gain is ever permanently lost. If one temporarily falls back into ordinary states of awareness, the previous realizations will be reclaimed. The constructive tendencies that have been acquired will impel one to aspire to complete liberation of consciousness, and accomplish it.

Did we have goals to be achieved before we incarnated?

Some souls have specific goals to achieve before they are incarnated. Most souls incarnate because they are somewhat confused and are attracted back to the physical realm because of their desires and subconscious inclinations. Even enlightened saints who live in the physical realm for many years are sometimes reluctant to leave it because they have become used to being here. This mild reluctance is similar to that of a caged bird or animal that, when offered its freedom, may not want to leave the confinement of the cage to which it has become adapted. The most compelling urge that inclines souls to learn and acquire experience is the innate desire to be fully awake.

If we don't need to reincarnate, can we choose to return to help others?

Some souls return to help others because it is their destiny to do so, their compassion or their sentimental feelings incline them to do it, or they feel it to be their duty. To want to come back to help others may be a noble impulse, but it may also interfere with one's spiritual progress. It is better to awaken to liberation of consciousness before considering a return to this realm to help others. What then happens will be in accord with the Divine will (intention).

What is the best way to prepare for eventual transition from the physical body?

The best way to prepare is to nurture spiritual awareness now. When we meditate until we are superconscious, we "die" to the world. When we are superconscious at all times, we are "free while embodied" and will permanently retain this state of awareness.

During my teenage and young adult years, I was frequently told that everything in the scripture that I read was literally true and was not to be doubted. Now that I know better, I still have feelings of guilt because of what I now believe as a result my improved understanding. How can I overcome and release these troublesome feelings?

Disregard what others said, or say, that is not true. Use your own powers of discriminative intelligence and intuition. As your understanding improves and innate knowledge emerges you will be able to easily discern the difference between fact and fiction. Memories of past false ideas and the feelings they elicited will fade and no longer be troublesome.

Some people say that Satan is a destructive influence, that hell is an actual place where unbelievers go for eternity, and that it is possible for souls to die (cease to exit). What is the origin of these ideas?

In the course of human history, people imagined a variety of unseen forces which they believed could influence human affairs. Not knowing any better, they described them as gods, demigods (half human, half divine), angels, demons, fairies, and ghosts. Some were considered to be benevolent; others were thought of as harmful. The Hebrew word *satan* means "obstructor" or "accuser." When the Old Testament was translated into Greek (early third century B.C.E.), the word was changed to *diabolus* (French *diable*, German *Teuful*, English *devil*). The first historical evidence of attempting to concentrate "evil" in a single personal form occurred around the sixth century B.C.E., in Persia. Zoroastrians used the name *Ahiriman* for a Principle of Darkness then erroneously believed to be engaged in ceaseless conflict with a Principle of Light for control of souls and the world. The concept of "personified evil" was adopted by Jewish religious thinkers and later by early Christians and others.

No reference to "hell" as a place for unrepentant souls is to be found in the Old Testament. The concept entered Jewish theology after 586 B.C.E. because of the influence of Persian dualism (belief in two realities and powers, divine and evil) which strongly influenced Jewish (and later) Christian and Muslim thinking. In the New Testament, the word *hell* is derived from the Valley of Gehinnom, a ravine south of Jerusalem which was formerly used by a pagan cult that practiced ritual child sacrifice. *Gehinnom* was translated in the Greek Bible, the Septuagint, as *Gehenna*, and in the New Testament as "hell." The spelling of the word comes from the Old Norse verb *helan*, "to hide"; in Norse mythology, before Christianity, *Hel* was said to be the goddess of death and the underworld.

Although theologians of various religious traditions have long pondered the matter of where to send errant souls after they leave this world, hell as an actual place does not exist. A Catholic Church definition of hell is a permanent state of being alienated (removed or isolated) from God—which is not possible.

In a recent poll, 60 percent of Americans who were questioned said they believed that Satan was real. Thirty percent affirmed a belief in hell, although most said they didn't believe they would go there. It is good to know that human opinions are fallible.

Do evil entities exist? If so, can they influence us?

An edition of Webster's Dictionary defines "evil" as that which is morally wrong or which causes injury, ruin, or pain. The word is related to the words *up* and *over* and to the prefix *hypo* (under, beneath). The basic sense of the word, which is no longer used, probably meant "exceeding proper bounds" or "overreaching," and did not signify the absence of good. Today, however, it is common to hear people refer to evil as a force or power that is in a contest with a good force or power. There is only one Power.

There are people whose actions cause misfortune for themselves and for others who are influenced by them. There is no need to be concerned about the intentions or actions of disembodied "entities," and the misguided intentions or actions of others who are in this world need not overly influence us. When we are established in Self-awareness and engaged in purposeful actions we are inclined to experience harmonious, supportive circumstances. There is no need to pray for protection from "evil" influences; the belief that this is necessary may cause mental and emotional conflicts that interfere with personal well-being and spiritual growth.

Do we have guardian angels that assist us?

The word *angel* is from Greek *angelos*, the equivalent of Hebrew *mal'akh*, "messenger." Angels were considered as "servants," "ministers," "watchers," or "holy ones set apart" from ordinary mortals. In the fifth century, Christian theologians borrowed from Jewish and Persian myths and imagined a hierarchy of "heavenly helpers."

A few years ago, seventy percent of the people in the United States who were asked if they believed in angels said yes. Fifty percent believed that they had a personal guardian angel and admitted to feeling more confident and safer because of their belief.

The belief in invisible spirits as agents of revelation or executors of divine will indicates that many people acknowledge that divine activities influence and effect human experience.

I am occasionally asked if a person on a spiritual path can believe in the existence of angels. We are free to have our opinions. Belief in popular ideas, however, is not the same as having accurate knowledge.

My concept of God is that of a supreme Consciousness devoid of personality attributes rather than a person. How can I pray and relate to it?

The prayer process works the same way regardless of

our concept (or understanding) of God. People who pray to God as a heavenly father or divine mother often report satisfying results. This does not mean that God is a cosmic person; only that one is able to pray and believe. Unwavering belief that one has what is desired or needed can cause it to manifest or can attract it. When praying for knowledge and experience of God, aspire to know, then be still and patiently wait. When the mind is calm, innate knowledge can emerge.

Some of my prayers produce results and some do not.

When praying: 1) know what to ask for; 2) pray until you know and feel at the core of your being that you have it. Some prayers do not produce desired results because we may pray unwisely even though we have good intentions. This is especially so when we pray for the welfare of others without knowing their desires, karmic condition, or destiny. When praying for our own purposes, we may be too insistent in wanting the results we imagine to be ideal without knowing what is best for us, or we may want a result that cannot occur in accord with natural laws of cause and effect. Keep a written record of what you pray for and write "fulfilled" beside the prayer theme when results occur. In this way you will be able to improve your prayer practice. Doing this will also increase your self-confidence. Sometimes, we have to do more than pray; we have to perform constructive actions. The axiom, "God helps those who help themselves," is useful to remember—and put into practice.

Can prayer be used along with meditation practice?

Pray to acknowledge the reality of God, request help in meditation practice, and focus attention on what you want to experience. As thoughts become settled, you can proceed to contemplation.

Define concentration and contemplation.

Concentration is focused attention. Contemplation is concentration on what one wants to experience or know *with expectation* of discovery. Passively sitting and thinking is not real contemplation. Contemplation requires keen interest and alert attention. When you want to experience deep peace or an awareness of God's presence, aspire to do so while being attentive to the changes that occur. When you want to know the truth about your real nature, God, or a metaphysical subject, aspire to know until insight emerges in your awareness. Although thoughts may arise and provide a partial understanding, what is wanted is knowledge acquired by direct insight or the emergence of innate knowledge. By regular, skillful practice of meditative contemplation, exceptional powers of perception and greatly improved functional abilities can be acquired.

Describe some useful meditation techniques.

The easiest way to meditate is to sit and be still until deep physical relaxation and mental calmness prevails. When you are meditating, it is helpful to have your awareness focused in the front, and upper, brain. When your mind is calm, contemplate your pure-conscious nature.

Techniques may include breath awareness; use of a word or word-phrase (mantra); pranayama; and other procedures. A mantra can be mentally recited, then mentally "listened to" to take attention into deeper levels of consciousness. It is of utmost importance to be alert and attentive when meditating.

Since some subjective perceptions that are produced by the mind or brain are similar to meditative perceptions, how can we know if what we perceive is of real value?

Meditative perceptions that clarify your awareness and enhance your ability to live more effectively are of value. Perceptions that distract you from the primary purpose of meditation practice or that do not result in clarification of awareness and improved ability to live effectively are useless.

Is meditating with others of value? Or should I instead focus on my private meditation practices?

Group meditation can be helpful if the participants are spiritually inclined. If group practice is helpful to you, participate. Also, maintain a schedule of private meditation practice. Avoid becoming dependent on the presence of others when you meditate.

When I meditate, I am sometimes able to immediately be in a calm, concentrated state. Should a meditation technique be practiced then, or later?

When you experience a calm, meditative state, let it persist. Use a meditation technique only to improve your concentration when necessary.

When meditating and settled in a thought-free state, what else should I do?

Just be there, aware and observant. Let your innate urge to be fully awake allow what occurs.

Gently aspire to realize your true Self as it is.

How can intuition be cultivated and improved?

Expect to be able to easily know what you want to know. Don't consider intuition as strange, unusual, or a special gift. Cultivate mental and emotional peace. Think and feel at the level of soul awareness. Avoid restless, superficial thinking, feelings, and behaviors. Meditate superconsciously on a regular schedule. As your innate powers of perception are unveiled, you will be pleased to notice that your intuition is more reliable. Mental and emotional peace and an almost effortless intention or inclination to know what you want to know allows intuition to more easily function. Avoid talking about your intuitive insights. To do so may invite meaningless conversation which may cause mental or emotional confusion.

When in need of guidance to make decisions or solve a problem, how can the difference between what seems to be intuitive insight and faulty reasoning be discerned?

What is intuitively perceived will be compatible with reasoned conclusions if one has access to facts which allow thinking to be rational. If objective evidence to support what seems to be intuitive insight is lacking, go slowly when making important decisions. When a solution to a problem is desired or needed, whenever possible, test what seems to be intuitive insight to verify it. When using intuition, it is best to avoid sentimental feelings and wishful thinking which may blur your awareness and interfere with rational thinking.

I have had some dreams that alerted me of future events. Can you comment on this?

When our awareness is not confined by the senses, it is possible to have precognitive insights when we are awake and when we dream. Not all dreams are related to the future; it is more usual that they occur when memories of perceptions and experiences are being processed and organized by the brain and mind. I, too, have had previews of future events while dreaming, although I usually "just know" the trends of events when I am awake.

How can I know when I am ready to commit to discipleship on a spiritual path?

You are ready for spiritual discipleship when you know in your heart (the essence of your being) that no other choice is as important to your well-being and spiritual growth. Some characteristics of a spiritual disciple are:

- Sincere willingness to learn and apply what is learned.
- Sufficient intellectual and intuitive capacity to comprehend what one needs to know.
- Sincere willingness to grow to emotional maturity and be responsible for thoughts, feelings, and behaviors.

- Respect for the teaching tradition.
- Respect for the teacher (if one has a teacher).
- Devoted (faithful) commitment to spiritual growth.

Discipleship is not for a person who prefers to be self-centeredly satisfied and undisciplined. If one is completely committed to learning and to awakening through the stages of spiritual growth, discipleship results in psychological transformation that allows spiritual growth to rapidly occur.

For success on the discipleship path, is it necessary to have a guru (spiritual teacher or mentor)?

The example, knowledge, guidance and encouragement of a spiritually aware teacher can be helpful. If a meaningful teacher-student relationship cannot be had, one can learn from books and other reliable sources. Right endeavors and the impulses of grace will then enable an ardent truth seeker to be successful on the spiritual path. An enlightened guru directs the disciple to God. It is the disciple's duty to do what is necessary to remove inner and outer obstacles to God-realization.

Of the many people who claim to be committed disciples on the spiritual path, only a few actually conform their lives to the principles, practices, and lifestyle regimens that should determine their thinking and actions. It is easy to *talk* about discipleship; what is important is to *demonstrate* it.

During my first private meeting with my guru, on a late Sunday afternoon, Christmas Day, December 25,

1949, after I verbally affirmed my commitment to the spiritual path, he recommended specific study and meditation practice routines that would be useful for me. He then advised: "Read a little; meditate more; think of God all the time."

During my last visit with him, approximately three weeks before he left his body, his final instruction was, "Don't look back. Don't look to the left or to the right. Go all the way in this lifetime. You can do it."

You, too, can take these words into your heart: the core of your being. They can inspire and motivate you to steadfastly persist on your awakening path.

Can I have a guru-disciple relationship with a teacher who is not physically embodied?

If your guru is not embodied and accessible, it is not possible to receive the instruction and guidance that is needed. Even though you may have a spiritual rapport with or be inspired by the written words or exemplary life of a deceased teacher, it is necessary to have reliable, direct communication with someone with whom you can personally interact.

If someone told you that they learned how to drive a car, prepare food, read or speak a foreign language, or manage their financial affairs by having telepathic communication with someone, you wouldn't believe it. In like manner, if a person believes that specific instruction is being given to them by someone who is not really with them, their belief is false. The cultivation of our innate, spiritual qualities is too important for us to waste our valuable time by being involved with fantasy.

What if I commit to discipleship, then fall back into former unwholesome routines and habitual behaviors?

Renew your commitment and go forward. Don't consider yourself to be unworthy or weak. As you persist, the former unwholesome or nonuseful habits will be replaced by good habits and you will be pleased with your progress.

Three actions are necessary if we are to succeed on the spiritual path.

- A decision must be made to be spiritually awake.
- Knowledge of how to do this must be acquired.
- Useful knowledge that is acquired must be used.

When the decision to be Self-realized is resolute and knowledge of what to do has been acquired and is wisely used, spiritual awakening will definitely occur. Firm resolve will empower you to be self-disciplined and to persist on your awakening path.

CHAPTER THREE

How to Know God

Ask, and it shall be given to you; seek, and you shall find; knock, and it shall be opened unto you. – *The Gospel of Matthew 7:7*

At the innermost level of your being, you are always pure, serene, and have knowledge of God and cosmic processes. It is only at surface levels of awareness that confusion can exist. The removal of confusion can be accomplished in the following ways:

- Rational thinking
- Using our powers of discriminative intelligence.
- Self-analysis to apprehend our true nature.
- Wholesome, orderly living.
- Meditating to relax the body and calm the mind, and sitting until a clear, superconscious state prevails.

Use your powers of discernment to be aware of the difference between yourself as a spiritual being and ordinary, modified states of awareness. This will enable you to be soul-centered and to observe your thoughts, emotional states, and outer conditions with an attitude of dispassionate objectivity. When you are God-realized, you will think rationally, live effectively, and maintain awareness of your real nature in relationship to the Infinite.

How to Naturally and Easily Awaken
Through the Stages of Spiritual Growth

The seven stages of spiritual growth experienced by souls as they awaken from ignorance of their true nature and God to illumination and liberation of consciousness can be discerned by observing their mental states and behaviors. Mental states and states of awareness are said to be related to vital centers (chakras) in the spine and brain.

The characteristics that correspond to stages of spiritual growth indicate the predominant state; characteristics of other states may also be present. Examples: a person who is only partially spiritually aware may sincerely aspire to a higher (more clarified) state of awareness; a person who is more spiritually aware may have mental attitudes and behavioral characteristics of lower (less clear) states of awareness.

#1. Unconscious of Spiritual Realities

Awareness is clouded and egocentric, completely identified with an mistaken sense of selfhood. The physical body that was born and will die may be believed to be one's real identity. Understanding of spiritual realities is minimal or lacking. If one is religious, prayers may be directed to an imagined deity. One may hope to have a heaven-like reward after living a good life. Lifestyle is usually based on opinions rather than on what is known. Ordinary activities are impelled by desires and whims. Thinking is flawed. Powers of intellectual discernment are weak. Memories and acquired habits usually influence mental attitudes, emotional states, and behaviors. Provincialism (small-mindedness) and self-righteousness may be evident. A tendency to be strongly attached to ideas, things, circumstances, and personal relationships is related to the first chakra at the base of the spine.

#2. Dysfunctional Ego-Consciousness

Confined by an illusional sense of selfhood, although dim awareness of higher realities may be had, the mind is confused, emotions are unstable, and behaviors are egocentric and erratic. Sentimental ideas and feelings, emotional attachments and dependency, and addictive and self-limiting behaviors are common. Fantasies about mundane matters and higher realities may be preferred over a desire to know facts. Subliminal drives and influences often dominate thoughts and feelings. If one is inclined to ponder spiritual realities, blind acceptance of religious beliefs which comfort the mind or fascination with psychic phenomena may be evident. If one prays or meditates, an inclination to elicit or indulge in pleasant moods or to acquire psychic abilities may be stronger than aspiration to experience authentic spiritual growth. Sentimental attraction is related to the second chakra at the sacral region of the spine.

#3. Functional Ego-Consciousness

Although an illusional sense of selfhood prevails, one may be capable of rational thinking, effectively relating to others, and accomplishing chosen purposes. Partial understanding of spiritual realities may be present. Spiritual aspiration may be mingled with a desire to acquire knowledge of metaphysical principles and have a relationship with God that might result in more comfortable personal circumstances. One may be inclined to practice meditation primarily for the purpose of obtaining psychological and physical benefits rather than to be Self- and God-realized. A sense of individualism and egocentric self-determinism may be obstacles to spiritual growth. Energetic will to accomplish purposes is related to the third chakra at the lumbar region of the spine.

#4. Superconsciousness

One's essence of being is intuitively discerned, and right endeavors make possible further purification of the mind and clarification of awareness which allow spiritual growth to spontaneously occur. Egocentricity weakens and diminishes as Self-knowledge increases. Ordinary activities are entirely constructive. Relationships are enjoyed without compulsion. Meditation is practiced superconsciously. Powers of intellect and intuition rapidly improve. One may be dedicated to spiritual discipleship. Purification of the mind and awareness is accelerated as superconscious influences become pronounced. Self-determined mastery of mental states, emotions, and sensory impulses is related to the fourth chakra at the dorsal region (between the shoulder blades) of the spine.

#5. Self-Realization and Cosmic Consciousness

One's essence of being is directly known and experienced as other than the ego, mind, or physical body. The processes of life from the field of pure existence to the material realm are intellectually and intuitively apprehended as one field of Consciousness in which its various aspects are interrelated. Metaphysical principles are studied to acquire knowledge and meditation is practiced to make the Self-realized state unwavering. Ordinary activities are appropriate and life-enhancing as determined by rational thinking and intuition. Extraordinary powers of perception and exceptional functional skills may be acquired, which can be used to live more effectively and quicken one's spiritual awakening. Calm discernment is related to the fifth chakra in the cervical region of the spine.

#6. God-Consciousness

The full reality of God is directly known and experienced. Metaphysical study and spiritual practice provide insights that confirm inner realizations and enable God-consciousness to be permanent. Innate knowledge of God emerges. Powers of concentration and will (intention) and aspiration to liberation of consciousness are related to the sixth chakra (spiritual eye center between and above the eyebrows) and front lobes of the brain.

#7. Liberation of Consciousness

At the first stage, although one is spiritually enlightened, subconscious influences may contribute to fluctuations of awareness and interfere with rational thinking. When the mind is purified on all levels, liberation is permanent. Delusions (erroneous ideas) and illusions are absent. Awareness is restored to wholeness. Transcendence is related to the seventh (crown) chakra in the higher brain.

To more easily and quickly awaken to a higher stage of spiritual awareness, aspire to do so and emulate the behaviors of role models who are at that stage or higher. Thus inspired and self-motivated, mentally "see" yourself as you aspire to be. As a spiritual being, the potential to accomplish your purposes is already within you. Use the knowledge and abilities you have while acquiring more knowledge and improving your skills. The more committed you are to spiritual growth—and your effective actions confirm your commitment—the more rapid it will be. Cultivate faith in your abilities and be receptive to the actions of grace which will be increasingly evident in your life.

An egocentric sense of selfhood, complacency, lack of self-confidence, and feelings of inadequacy confine soul awareness and inhibit natural spiritual growth. Replace these conditions with Self-awareness, enthusiasm, unwavering Self-confidence, and faith in your ability to skillfully accomplish purposes which are of value to you.

- Adhere to a well-ordered, wholesome lifestyle to enjoy a long, healthy span of physical life that will enable you to fulfill your duties and accomplish your purposes.
- Accurately define your understanding of your true nature and God. Acknowledge that you are a spiritual being and discern the difference between God and God's attributes.

- Don't worry about current events that come and go. Focus your attention and actions on right living, acquiring higher knowledge, and spiritual practices.
- Live constructively with a clear sense of purpose. If you do not yet have a clear sense of purpose, pray for inspiration and use your creative imagination.
- Renounce nonessential activities and relationships.
- Cultivate optimism.
- Study to acquire knowledge of natural laws of cause and effect that operate in this realm and knowledge of your true nature in relationship to God. Concentrate only on what is true. When possible, skillfully use the knowledge you acquire to verify its usefulness.
- Meditate every day to become proficient in eliciting states of superconsciousness.

The Pure Stillness That Allows Self- and God-Knowledge to be Experienced

Meditative contemplation is a preparatory practice. When changes no longer occur in the mind, our true nature and the reality of God can be known. When we are engaged in contemplation, a sense of "otherness" remains. Oneness is realized when contemplation is transcended. Self-realization is knowing what we are rather than having a concept of what we are. God-realization is knowing what God is rather than imagining God as other than the one field of Consciousness.

Superconscious states experienced before Self-realization is experienced are impure, unstable, and modified by mental and emotional influences. When the mind and emotions are calm, absolute (pure) stillness allows Self- and God-knowledge to be directly apprehended.

During sleep, our awareness is usually identified with subconscious and unconscious states. When meditating, we internalize our attention to experience superconscious states.

Internalize your attention by withdrawing awareness from the senses to the spine, then to the higher brain. If this cannot be easily done, use this simple method:

Be aware of your spine (feel it), then go upward through the chakras from the base of the spine, sacral chakra, lumbar chakra, dorsal chakra, cervical chakra, spiritual eye and front region of the brain, and higher brain. Mentally chant "Om" or "God" at each chakra as you take your awareness upward and your attention flows inward. When awareness is established in the higher brain, sit still and patiently observe. Meditation will spontaneously occur.

Although preliminary superconscious states which are modified by mental influences can be enjoyable to experience and may provide useful insights, they are to be transcended in favor of Self- and God-realization.

Until you are established in a pure superconscious state, your attention may sometimes be distracted by thoughts and feelings that arise or perceptions of subjective phenomena that are seen or felt. Whatever is perceived, passively ignore. Eventually, subliminal influences will be calmed, your mind will be peaceful, and your awareness will be clear. When attention is completely internalized, your senses no longer convey information to the brain. Subliminal influences are absent, your mind is calm, and your awareness does not have any support. Innate knowledge of your true nature can then spontaneously emerge, and prevail.

You are Destined to Be Spiritually Enlightened

Regardless of your present stage of spiritual growth, until you are Self- and God-realized, continue to aspire to be fully awake. Avoid comparing your progress with that of others. Don't talk about your insights or meditative experiences with anyone except your teacher or mentor, if you have one. Just concentrate on what you need to do to allow your spiritual awakening to be rapid and satisfying. Rational thinking, right (wholesome) living, and right spiritual practice will remove (and enable you to rise above) all obstacles to your innate urge to have your awareness fully restored to wholeness.

A major obstacle to spiritual growth is passive acceptance of existing oppressive conditions. When our awareness is *ordinary*, we may think that nothing can be done to improve our circumstances or consider them to be normal because they are commonly experienced by others with whom we associate. Mental confusion, emotional instability, and lack of self-confidence are normal characteristics when we are identified with the human condition. Orderly, rational thinking, emotional stability, clarity of awareness, and courage are normal characteristics when we are Self-motivated on the spiritual path.

Think, feel, and act in ways which enhance your life and support your desire to be spiritually awake. Do your best to avoid thoughts, moods, behaviors, and relationships that are not wholesome or do not support your spiritual aspirations. Consider everything that you do from moment-to-moment and day-to-day as spiritual practice that is as helpful in assisting your awakening through the stages of spiritual growth as are your regular interludes of meditative contemplation.

You are destined to be spiritually enlightened. Decide now to awaken to that free state during your present incarnation.

Affirmation

I know that God is my life and that my
major purpose is to be fully awake in God.
Forsaking all unimportant matters,
I remain dedicated to God-realization.

Answers to Questions About
How to Know God

Of the various obstacles to spiritual growth, what is a common obstacle to overcome?

Complacency—because of disinterest in spiritual growth or an inclination (or personal choice) to identify with ordinary human conditions. Replace complacency with curiosity about higher realities, aspiration to actualize your innate potential, and unwavering Self-knowledge-based-confidence that will enable you to know all that you can know and be all that you can be. For you, and for everyone who is highly motivated, the possibilities for learning and awakening are limitless. Be an active participant in the drama of life rather than be satisfied with ordinary circumstances.

I am not as attentive to my duties and spiritual practices as I would like to be because I am often concerned about disturbing events which are unpleasant to think about. What is the best way to think about, and relate to, world conditions?

As one of more than six billion people in the world, it is unlikely that you will be personally harmed by events that you read or hear about. You may experience some temporary effects of fluctuating economic conditions that reflect the moods and behaviors of others. When meditating, direct all of your attention to your practice. When not meditating, nurture Self- and God-awareness. Because you now abide in God, all is well with you.

Although I am regular in my spiritual practices, I feel that I am far from my goal of Self-realization. What should I do?

Analyze your concept of *time*. Think of it as a field, like space, in which events occur. At the innermost level of your being, you are knowledgeable and free; gently acknowledge this as true and be more aware of the essence of your being. What you desire to realize in the future already exits, to be acknowledged and actualized now.

I still have a few minor habits (consuming too much sugar is one) that I know are not constructive. What is the best way to overcome them?

Replace them with good habits. Don't be overly concerned about minor things. Be more purposeful; concentrate on what is important; ignore what is not important. Cultivate a more cosmic conscious outlook.

I would like to do something to assist others to well-being and spiritual growth, but do not know how to do this. What can I do that will be helpful?

Nurture your own well-being and spiritual growth. Your Self-realization and clarified awareness will then blend with the collective consciousness of everyone on the planet and beneficially influence it. When you know of someone who is interested in spiritual well-being, give them helpful literature. If they are sincere, they will respond to it.

I want to progress rapidly on the spiritual path. Is it necessary to "renounce the world" or to live a cloistered life to awaken quickly through the stages of spiritual growth?

There is no need to withdraw from society. What is useful is to discern the difference between your true Self and that to which you relate. In this way you can live effectively without being strongly attached to anything. Relate appropriately to others while allowing them the freedom to express in accord with their needs and inclinations. Perform all duties skillfully and fulfill personal obligations without mental or emotional attachment to what you do or the results of your actions. Live simply. When possible, avoid situations that may complicate your life or distract you from your major purposes. Maintain a daily schedule of quiet, meditative reflection. Once or twice a year it can be helpful to enjoy a private spiritual retreat for mental, physical, and spiritual renewal.

I am sincere in my desire to be fully, spiritually awake. Some members of my family, and others with whom I must interact at work and in my community, do not share my aspirations. Is this a major problem or obstacle?

While it is enjoyable to have personal relationships which are supportive of our spiritual aspirations, there is no need to depend on others to either understand our personal goals or to encourage them. The spiritual path is one of "aloneness" because others cannot really know what is occurring within us. Be outwardly attentive and appropriate to the needs of others while privately attending to those matters which are helpful to your continued learning and growing.

Can it be helpful to imagine what it will be like to be spiritually enlightened?

Since it is natural for us to imagine what might be possible to achieve or accomplish in the course of our lives, it can be helpful to also imagine what it would be like to be spiritually enlightened. Imagining what can be possible improves our receptivity to it. It can also inspire and motivate us.

Your Personal Spiritual Growth Program

What do you need to do to nurture your spiritual growth?

_____

_____

_____

_____

_____

_____

_____

Write a clearly defined affirmation that declares your intention and resolve.

_____

_____

_____

_____

CHAPTER FOUR

Living in God

I have not so far left the coasts of life to travel inland that I cannot hear the murmur of the Outer Infinite.

— Elizabeth Barrett Browning

As you continue to awaken through the stages of spiritual growth, you will have revealing insights that will illumine your mind and personal experiences that will confirm that you are on your right path in life.

Be alert and attentive to where you are in time and space and to what is occurring around you. Live your life as the immortal, spiritual being you are, knowing that the wholeness of God extends to where you are and that the material things you use and to which you relate are formed of God's cosmic forces. See everyone with whom you interact and think about as spiritual beings. Look past their surface characteristics and silently acknowledge their essence, which is the same as your own. The only differences between individuals are their outer appearance, personality characteristics, and states of mind and awareness. No one is above or below you. At the soul level, all are equally divine. Nurture and express your own divine qualities and the divine qualities of others.

Be purposeful in your thoughts and actions and decisive when making wise choices. You will have abundant energy and always be enthusiastic (infused with the spirit [life essence] of God). You will be physically healthy, mentally alert and peaceful, happy, prosperous in every way, and successful in all of your meaningful endeavors.

The more effectively you live, the faster your spiritual progress will be. The optimism, improved abilities, powers of concentration, and concentrated intention that enable you to live effectively, will also enable you to be successful in your endeavors to be Self- and God-realized.

Self-centered, pessimistic, purposeless individuals who do not yet have the will to live effectively, who allow themselves to be victimized by subliminal influences, harmful habits, addictive tendencies, and mundane circumstances, do not experience obvious spiritual growth because they are not receptive to it. While everyone has the same innate potential, the capacity to learn and grow has to be nurtured so that authentic spiritual growth can occur.

How to Always Have Peace of Mind in a Changing World

World conditions are ever being transformed, and transformation results in changes to which we have to adapt if we are to participate consciously and creatively with the ongoing processes of evolution. How we relate to events that occur and how we choose to live determine the degree of well-being and peace of mind we experience.

It is easy to be mentally and emotionally calm when our personal circumstances are orderly and predictable. It is not always so easy to be soul-centered and optimistic when events beyond our ability to control challenge our self-confidence and elicit thoughts and feelings that cause anxiety and stress.

The brain centers that regulate the body's reaction to threat or reward prompt us to avoid danger and perform actions which are necessary for our survival. When events that occur or are thought about are perceived as potentially dangerous, a fear response is triggered which signals the pituitary and adrenal glands to release hormones into the bloodstream that temporarily heighten awareness and prepare the body to react to real or imagined threats to its well-being.

When danger is averted, a problem related to survival is solved, or a goal related to survival is achieved, stress hormones are reduced. When the body is constantly stressed, the continuous exposure to adrenaline can damage the heart and cortisol can depress the immune system. Prolonged stress can damage the brain and result in headaches, back and neck pain, insomnia, disorientation, and feelings of hopelessness, tiredness, and despair for which no physical causes can be found. These symptoms, which are commonly experienced by some people who have difficulty coping with challenges confronted in their ordinary, everyday circumstances, are being increasingly observed in many people who are fearful and worried.

There are constructive actions we can perform that can enable us to manage stress, be mentally calm, emotionally stable, and effectively productive.

- Be goal-oriented, forward-looking, and intentional.
- Adhere to a wholesome dietary regimen (vegetarian is

best). Avoid harmful foods and beverages.

- Exercise regularly: lift weights, walk, swim, practice hatha yoga or tai chi.
- View events and circumstances objectively.
- Don't talk about events that trouble your mind or may cause others to be fearful or worried. Replace negative thoughts with positive thoughts.
- Maintain a regular schedule of purposeful activity and adequate rest. Confident living elicits feelings of mental and emotional satisfaction that neutralize thoughts, feelings, and memories of fear and uncertainty.
- Cultivate optimism by expecting the best possible outcome for situations that are unfolding in your life and in the world. Remember that the universe has existed for approximately 14 billion years, our planet has existed for 4 billion years, and human beings have prevailed for at least one million years. The trends and forces of evolution are supportive of nature, and us.
- Meditate daily to elicit deep relaxation that reduces stress, calms the mind and emotions, and allows your awareness to be clarified.

Do all of the practical things while nurturing your awareness of the Presence of God. You are responsible for your personal circumstances; God is responsible for the ongoing processes of life. The more soul- and God-conscious you are, the easier it will be for you to live effectively and have what is needed for your total well-being. *An enlivening Power is nurturing the universe and you can learn to cooperate with it.*

When you are worried and feelings of uncertainty arise, remove your attention from objective circumstances for a while and be soul-centered. At the innermost level of your being you are serene and secure. Here, you can know that you abide in the wholeness of God. You can be peaceful and fearless. Cultivate unwavering soul-awareness and radiate soul peace to others.

The quiet place within you is immediately accessible by directing your attention to it. Here, you can rest and be renewed and strengthened. Daily sit in the silence until you are consciously aware of your oneness with God. After meditation, maintain your Self- and God-awareness as you attend to your duties and nurture personal relationships—knowing that you are God-supported and God-provided at all times.

Live up to your full potential by concentrating only on important matters, improving your skills and abilities, and living effectively. You are an immortal, spiritual being in the world to discover the truth about yourself and your relationship to the Infinite, cultivate and actualize your divine qualities, fulfill your higher purposes, and nurture others and the planet. Live like the immortal, spiritual being you are.

In every personal relationship—and when you think of others, regardless of who, or where, they are—acknowledge their innate divine nature and noble qualities. As units of one Reality, we share a common essence and a common destiny. See through all outer appearances of conditions to *That* which is forever real and reliable.

*You Can Experience the Prospering Power of a
Positive Mental Attitude Supported by Rational
Thinking and Intentional Constructive Actions*

You can do it because you are a spiritual being abiding in the ocean of infinite Consciousness, your mind is one with Universal Mind, and almost unlimited creative potential is within you.

We truly prosper when the spiritual, mental, emotional, physical, and environmental components of our lives are harmoniously integrated. Are you prospering in all aspects of your life? If you are not yet prospering in every way, *you should — and can do it*!

- *Prosper spiritually* by acknowledging your divine nature and your relationship with God. Clarify your awareness; meditate daily to the stage of superconsciousness. Be soul-centered and live as the spiritual being you really are. You are *in* God now. Nurture awareness of the reality of God's presence.

- *Prosper mentally* by thinking rationally, creatively, and optimistically. The mental states you choose to maintain, the thoughts you habitually think, the feelings you nurture, and your conscious or subliminal desires are manifesting as your experiences and circumstances. You are experiencing the natural outcomes of universal, impersonal laws of cause and effect and you can learn to cooperate with them.

- *Prosper emotionally* by being objectively insightful in regard to what you observe, how you react to events that occur, and by having ideal, harmonious circumstances that provide you with peace of mind and feelings of security. Learn to have your life-enhancing desires and real needs easily satisfied. Cultivate soul-contentment regardless of external conditions. Control your moods. Nurture happiness and self-confidence.

- *Prosper physically* by cultivating a "health consciousness," obtaining sufficient sleep, and maintaining a balance of activity and rest. Maintain your ideal body weight. Manage stress. Remember that mental and emotional states also influence your physical health. Drink pure water and breathe fresh air. Schedule some time outside every day to obtain the benefits of natural light.
- *Prosper in your relationships* by wisely choosing to have and nurture relationships that are harmonious and supportive. See the divine nature in every person while being selective in your choices of frequent or long-term relationships. Compatible ideals and purposes are more likely to result in mutually beneficial relationships.
- *Prosper in your endeavors* by defining your worthwhile goals and purposes, creative use of imagination, improving your intellectual powers, and wise, disciplined use of your knowledge and skills. Acquire more knowledge and skills as necessary.
- *Prosper in all ways* by nurturing Self- and God-awareness and improving your capacity to vividly imagine, firmly believe, and thankfully accept all of the good fortune that is possible for you to have.

When thinking, planning, interacting with others, working, or creatively performing your chosen or necessary duties—do it in relationship with the Source of everything. Interact with the It and allow It to provide for you.

Use the following affirmation to elevate your mind and awareness above all thoughts and feelings of limitation to a clear, superconscious level of complete acknowledgment and acceptance of what you are thinking and saying. Affirm from the innermost core of your being:

Yes, I am now prospering in all aspects of my life!

Speak it aloud three times *with conviction.*
Three times with *increasing conviction.*
Three times, knowing and *feeling it to be so.*
Three times with *vivid realization.*
Be still. *Superconsciously accept your fulfillment.*

There is no magic involved in affirming three times at each level. Affirm as many times as you feel inclined. Rejoice in the transformational experience that results from mental renewal, clarification of awareness, and enlivening surges of energy. Think, feel, live, and act from that level of consciousness from now on.

Now is the most favorable moment in time to decide to know God and do what is necessary to allow your innate knowledge to emerge. Do not waver in your resolve to have your awareness fully restored to wholeness by your own right endeavors and God's supportive grace.

Answers to Questions About Living in God

What is the best way to choose and achieve goals?

Think in terms of your needs and having them met. Decide what you want to do or accomplish. Make choices based on what seems to you to be the best or most meaningful goals. Assess the knowledge, skills, and abilities you have that can enable you to achieve your goals.

- Clearly define your goals by writing them in order of importance or usefulness.
- Write a specific plan of action that will enable you to progressively achieve them.
- Vividly imagine the end results, believing that what you need, or want to achieve, is certain to manifest.
- Do the practical things that can be done to have your needs met and your goals achieved.
- If you do not know what to do, maintain unwavering faith in the outcome, knowing that Universal Mind is responsive to your needs and desires.
- Be alert and attentive to all possibilities of unplanned good fortune that can emerge.

Daily, after you meditate and are peaceful, *desire with gentle intention* to have what is needed or wanted. *Know and feel at the core of your being that you already have it.* After your meditation session, calmly maintain that con-

viction. When you are established in Self- and God-awareness, needs will be spontaneously met and desires will be
easily fulfilled.

What is the recommended diet for a person who is on a
spiritual path? Is it necessary to be a vegetarian?

Choose a variety of wholesome, natural foods only in
the quantity that is needed. Excessive eating burdens the
body's systems and may contribute to disease. A high
percentage of physical ailments are directly related to
improper diet (some cancers, heart problems, strokes, dia-
betes, and others). A low calorie (sufficient but not excessive) nutrition-rich diet can be useful for persons who want
to enjoy a healthy, long life. A vegetarian diet is recommended. Ideal body weight should also be maintained.
Use common sense in matters of diet.

Although I very much like the idea of prospering in all
aspects of my life, it has been difficult for me to have enough
money. I am aware of a deep-seated resistance to having
money and some of the other material things that I need
or want.

There is no virtue in being impoverished. There is an
abundance of necessary material resources in our universe. You should have what you need, or want, so that
you can be comfortable and accomplish all of your purposes which are of value. When you have a surplus of
money, you will be able to support social, cultural, and
spiritual endeavors for the good of others.
    When you become aware of thoughts or feelings of limi-

tation, let them go. You are a spiritual being living in God. You deserve to be prosperous and have access to all of the material resources that you need.

Use these affirmations:

> My constant, conscious awareness of my
> true nature as a spiritual being in relationship
> with the Infinite is my assurance of orderly,
> timely unfoldments of resources and supportive
> events, circumstances, and relationships that
> are always continuously and appropriately
> provided for my highest good.

> The enlivening Spirit of God is freely expressive in
> and through me. It illumines my mind, regenerates my
> body, removes all restrictions to its flow, inspires me
> with creative ideas, empowers my constructive actions,
> and harmoniously arranges all of my circumstances
> and relationships for my highest good.
> All aspects of my life are now in divine order.

Improve your understanding until you are fully aware that spiritual and material realities are two aspects of one Reality. God is the Source of everything. For what is provided for you from the Source, be thankful. Do all of the practical things that you know to do to help yourself to be more prosperous. Wisely manage money and other material resources while being receptive to more of what you need or desire to have.

Consider all that you do as useful spiritual practice. Pray (wish) for the prosperity, total well-being, and spiritual fulfillment of everyone. Be happy when you see others prosper.

*What is the difference between superconscious affirmation
and using affirmations to reprogram or condition the subconscious mind?*

Superconscious affirmation enables us to know at the
deepest level of our being the truth of what we affirma-
tively acknowledge. We can then live from that state of
realization.

Subconscious conditionings, memories, habits, and
addictive tendencies that may interfere with rational
thinking and endeavors to live effectively are resisted,
weakened, and neutralized by superior superconscious
realizations. When we see (in our mind) and soulfully feel
the reality of new, life-enhancing possibilities, the mind
accepts as true what is vividly imagined. The subconscious
mind records perceptions; it does not discriminate between
what is perceived through the five senses and what is
imagined as being real.

When we think, act, and react to events in accord with
subconscious influences, our thoughts, actions, and reactions are effects of those influences. When we think and
perform actions superconsciously, what we do is always
spontaneously appropriate.

*Although I try to remain Self- and God-aware, I tend to be
easily influenced by the opinions and behaviors of others,
assume their mental attitudes, and often become involved
in activities and relationships which are not useful. What
can I do to be more self-reliant?*

Begin each day with prayer and meditation. Read a
selection from an inspired source to nourish your mind

with positive ideas. Be appropriate when relating to others while being objective. You will then be able to be more *Self*-reliant and discerning. When possible, have friends and associates who are as purposeful as you desire to be.

Does living in God mean that I cannot also live a normal life?

Living in God means that you can live a *natural* life. What is usually considered to be "normal" are behaviors which are habitual for most people who are not yet sincerely interested in having a relationship with God.

Living in God will enable you to live more effectively and enjoyably and have meaningful relationships. Every day will provide opportunities for discovery. As your understanding blossoms, you will see the world in a new and different way and know God, as God is, more fully.

How can we know our real purpose in life and be sure that what we do is worthwhile?

Our ultimate purpose in life is to be so fully awake in God that our consciousness is liberated from false ideas and conditionings. While we are still awakening, we should live constructively and responsibly attend to our duties. The work we do should benefit us and others whose lives are influenced by it. It is helpful to be mindful that our habitual mental states and prevailing states of awareness also influence the collective consciousness of all people and living things.

If you are not yet certain that you are "in your right place" in life, calmly think about the matter until ideas surface in your mind that seem worthy of consideration, or events occur that provide opportunities that seem worthy of further examination.

Be a possibility-thinker. Ask, "Why am I here?" and "What can I do that will be of value?" Write the ideas as they arise in your mind. Then look at what you wrote and mark the ideas that seem useful to consider. When you decide on what you think to be best for you, write some plans for implementing your projects. While you are doing this, be aware that you are in God and that your mind is one with God's omnipresent mind. Think and feel that you are one of God's agents on earth, because you are, as is every person. The more conscious you are of your relationship with the Infinite—and think and act in harmonious accord with its inclinations—the more certain you will be that you are doing what is right for you. You will always be enthusiastic (God-inspired) and supportive events and circumstances will unfold in ways that you could not have imagined.

During my teenage years, I intuitively knew that I was here to awaken in God and to inform others about how they, too, could be awake in God. Surrendered to this clear sense of destiny, of the role I was to play, I prayed for guidance and acquired information that I felt would be useful. Within a few years, I met my guru, studied further, meditated deeply, was ordained before my twenty-first year, and have been teaching and serving since then. Almost all useful events that have occurred have been due to God's grace. I have, of course, done my part to perform effective actions, yet God's grace has played the most influential role.

Firmly convinced that we are in this world to serve, I have always been willing to do it. The following excerpt from a longer poem by Alfred Lord Tennyson (1809 – 1892) inspires me, as I hope it will inspire you:

> Well, I dreamed
> That stone by stone I rear'd a sacred
> fane,
> A temple, neither Pogod, Mosque, nor
> Church,
> But loftier, simpler, always open-door'd
> To every breath from heaven, and Truth
> and Peace
> And Love and Justice came and dwelt
> therein.
>
> *– Akbar's Dream*

Shortly after I began to travel and teach, during the late 1950s, I became aware of being supported, guided, and provided for by the "benevolent Power" that I had always felt and known during my childhood and later years. When I needed to do something that I had never done before, when I imagined it as it would be when it was actual or real, I either intuitively knew what to do, or events would emerge that would make possible the desired outcome. I learned that self-reliance is, in the words of Ralph Waldo Emerson, "reliance on God."

Cultivate Self-confidence: faith in what you are as a unit of God's being. Nurture awareness of the presence of God. Be willing to do your utmost to accomplish the purposes that seem to you to be of real value. Consider your life as a great adventure, then go forward.

I feel that I commune with God when I meditate and thoughts of God are almost always in the background of my mind. I have a few personal problems to overcome and situations that are not as harmonious as I would like for them to be. Can you provide me with guidance in regard to solving these problems and having harmony in my relationships?

Define the problem or troublesome condition, imagine an ideal solution for it, then do what can be done to overcome it. If physical healing is needed, *imagine* and *feel* that you are vibrantly healthy and attend to practical matters (nutritious diet, exercise, and rest). Obtain professional advice and treatment if necessary. If you need to be prosperous, nurture a "prosperity consciousness" and act in accord with it. If you are not inwardly peaceful or are anxious, worried, or have some mental and emotional conflicts, cultivate rational thinking and self-confidence. Go deep into your being and live from that awareness.

Do what you can to fairly and appropriately resolve unpleasant situations. If your efforts are not successful, consider removing yourself from inharmonious situations and/or relationships. Remember that you have the freedom to make wise choices and you deserve to be healthy, happy, comfortable, secure, and fulfilled.

Although I am doing my best to live a God-centered life, some people I know tell me that I should go to their church and are trying to convert me to their religious beliefs. How can this situation be appropriately resolved?

The easy way to solve this problem is to avoid discussions about religious beliefs or practices. If others persist in their attempts to persuade you to accept their religious beliefs, tell them, nicely, that you prefer not to talk about the matter. If they still persist, avoid them.

Some people, whose rigid, fundamentalist religious beliefs dominate their lives, feel it to be their duty to convert others to their views. This behavior is more obvious among members of religious groups who share a strong conviction of infallibility in regard to their beliefs and practices.

I am doing my best to live in God and feel that I have several more years to live in my present incarnation, yet I sometimes feel detached from mundane circumstances and have little or no attraction to most things that seem to appeal to people I know. I wonder if I am becoming too other-worldly?

It is not necessary to be attracted to what appeals to people whose awareness is ordinary or who are not sincerely interested in spirituality. Since you have several more years to live in this world, why not think in terms of what you might do that would be of interest to you as well as of value to others? If you have experience, knowledge, skills, or material resources that can be used to benefit others and the planet, selflessly serve as you think to be best, without need for special recognition or thoughts or feelings of pride.

Be curious about life and what there is yet to learn and do. Exercise your mind as well as your body. Acquire new skills. Challenge your intellect. Expand your consciousness. Be attentive to what occurs in your world. Express your creative powers. Be innovative: do new things or do ordinary things in a different, useful way.

Wherever you are in space-time you will have to relate to your environment. Do it skillfully.

My intellectual understanding of spiritual realities comforts my mind, yet I often feel lonely and insecure. What can be done to overcome these feelings?

Having an intellectual understanding of spiritual realities is useful; flawless comprehension of them is redemptive. When you are established in Self- and God-awareness, you will not feel lonely or insecure. Cultivate Self-respect and Self- and God-awareness. It might also be helpful to analyze your feelings of loneliness and insecurity and observe the thoughts and memories that are mixed with those feelings. Be receptive to compatible relationships without allowing strong feelings of need to cause you to make unwise choices. Avoid behaving in nonuseful or erratic ways in a frantic attempt to compensate for thoughts or feelings of loneliness or insecurity. Avoid preoccupation with debilitating thoughts and feelings. Don't talk about personal problems. Concentrate attention and energies on meaningful endeavors. Maintain a regular schedule of meditation practice. Frequently remind yourself that, in God, your peace of mind and complete well-being are assured. Whatever then unfolds in your personal life will be ideal.

I have a very busy work and social schedule and am inclined to become so outwardly involved that I become hyperactive and am not always able to think or act rationally or quickly make right decisions. What can I do to be more calm and to function more effectively?

Begin each day with meditation practice. Write a list of your work and social schedules in the order of their importance. Attend to important matters first. Cancel or minimize the projects and relationships which are not necessary or are not of value.

When you notice that you are too emotionally reactive or your mind is restless, sit still in a quiet place until you are centered in Self- and God-awareness. You will then be able to calmly attend to your duties and more easily make right decisions. Affirm (know with certainty):

Every thought I have, every action I perform,
every event that occurs, every situation with which
I am involved, is now in divine order.

My family and work obligations are so demanding of my time and energy that I sometimes think I should wait until I retire to devote myself to spiritual study and practice. What do you think about this matter?

It would be a mistake to wait. Meditate every day, if only for half an hour. Read a portion from an inspired source to nourish your mind with wholesome, positive ideas. Reduce your obligations to others while fulfilling those which are of value. Your increased spiritual awareness will enable you to be more skillful and efficient while allowing time for nurturing family relationships.

Procrastination (delaying until later what should be done now) may prevent you from having the fulfillment you deserve. You do not know now what your future circumstances will be if you neglect the nurturing of your spiritual well-being at your present stage in life. Aspire to God-realization. Integrate your spiritual growth endeavors with your other activities.

Some philosophers and scientists assert that the emergence of life on our planet was "accidental" and that human beings are of no more significance than any of the less complex forms of life. Are our lives meaningful, or not?

Our being here *is* significant: meaningful and important in the cosmic order. Planet Earth may not have been predestined to nurture life forms but it so happened that conditions here were ideal for their emergence and evolution. Our planet is ideally positioned in space in relationship to the sun for life to prevail. It is neither too hot nor too cold and has the chemical components, moisture, air, and atmosphere that allow living things to flourish. Millions of years ago, when conditions were supportive, consciousness was unveiled and simple organisms appeared. More complex forms of life evolved over a long period of time and humankind emerged. We, and everything, came from "inner space" and to there we will eventually return. While we are here, we can play a useful role in the continuing drama of life. Our bodies and minds are sufficiently evolved to enable the processing of higher states of consciousness.

It is not uncommon to read, or otherwise hear about,

the comments of "informed thinkers" who declare that
science and spirituality are in opposition, that they are
two distinct fields of interest to be investigated. This opinion is not reasonable; when both scientific and spiritual
research results in complete discovery of what is to be
known, what is revealed will be the same.

Note: The word *man*, when used in the generic sense (describ-
ing a group or class with shared characteristics or traits), is
derived from Sanskrit *manas*, to think.

Do you think that conditions on the planet will improve?

The trend of evolution is causing orderly transformations of planetary conditions and is supportive of our constructive endeavors. Strife, conflicts, and most hardship
and suffering are caused by the irrational thinking and
faulty behaviors of people who are not yet spiritually
awake.

Conditions on our planet have been dramatically improved during the past two hundred years, and this trend
is certain to continue. Don't allow any "prophets of doom"
to poison your mind with their unenlightened opinions.
Cultivate optimism, improve your understanding, and
make your own creative and useful contributions to the
well-being of our world.

*I have decided to live up to my full potential in regard to
being effectively functional in all that I do and to be Self-
and God-realized in this incarnation. What can you recommend that will enable me to do this?*

Do not waver in your resolve. Be responsible for what

you think, feel, and do. Acquire the knowledge you need to have to accomplish your purposes and wisely use it.

To live effectively, define your goals, concentrate on what is necessary for you to do, and eliminate what is not necessary. Decide on the best use of time and resources: decide how much to time you will devote to metaphysical study and meditation practice; family responsibilities; community service; work and social interactions; recreation; and whatever else needs to be done. Wisely manage money and other material resources.

Write a list of goals, why you have chosen them, and how you can most efficiently achieve them. Write a list of your meaningful purposes, why they are important to you, and how you intend to accomplish them.

To quickly awaken to Self- and God-realization, cultivate awareness of your true nature and the reality of God. You are in God now; acknowledge, contemplate, and fully apprehend (understand) that this is so.

Renounce all childishly dependent thoughts and emotions regarding your relationship with God. During the early stages of your spiritual growth, it is acceptable to pray, or endeavor to relate, to God however you imagine God to be. As you awaken through the stages of spiritual growth, you will become aware of what God is.

Can we heal ourselves of a disease or other physical problems by improving our spiritual understanding?

Because of knowing the relationship between soul, mind, and body, I believe that any physical problem can be healed. Improving our spiritual understanding is helpful, as is doing the practical, necessary things to restore the mind-body constitution to a balanced state.

It has been estimated that many of the illnesses that are commonly experienced are related to mental and emotional conflicts, improper diet, insufficient exercise, obesity, environmental pollution, and unsanitary living conditions. It is also believed that seventy percent of the causes of illness and sudden-death episodes (heart attack, strokes, accidents) that contribute to premature death can be avoided.

Spiritual understanding enables us to more easily manage stress, have peace of mind, and be emotionally calm. Also, when we are spiritually conscious, we are more likely to adhere to a more wholesome lifestyle.

In many parts of the world where "modern" eating and other lifestyle habits have been adopted, physical problems that are common in modern societies become increasingly evident.

Spiritual understanding, a strong will to be healthy and functional; orderly, optimistic thinking; emotional stability; a nutritious diet, appropriate exercise; and clean environmental conditions are supportive of our health and well-being. When the immune system is strong, the body is more disease-resistant.

For healing, and to stay healthy, we can help ourselves by cultivating spiritual awareness and adopting useful, health-promoting habits. If professional help is needed, this should also be included.

It is necessary to tithe in order to prosper?

To *tithe* is to freely give ten percent. Doing this is encouraged by some religious groups as a way to ensure a flow of money and material resources to maintain and expand the services that are provided for members of the group and for others who may also be served. If you are a member of a church or another organized religious body, be as generous as possible in supporting its activities. It is not necessary to adhere to a ten percent giving plan. If your financial resources are limited, give in accord with your available means and inclination, volunteer your skills, and in other ways be helpful. If you have an abundance of money, be generous, yet wise, in your choices of where and for what purpose you give.

Tithing as a way of improving one's consciousness of prosperity is often recommended because 1) those who recommend it believe that it works; 2) they are already prosperous; 3) they may want some of your money. I have known many individuals who said they tithed and "it didn't work" for them. They only way tithing can be effective in regard to having an increase of money or other resources is if generous, wise giving causes us to be more receptive to good fortune. It is then our faith, expectation, and (perhaps) wiser use of our skills and available resources that produce the results.

When using or giving money or any material thing, do it with the understanding that, *in* God, you *have* and *will always will have*, all that you need. Your constant, conscious awareness of the reality of God is the source of everything that is needed for your well-being. With this knowing, you will perform right actions, achieve goals, and easily attract the necessary resources and supportive events, circumstances, and relationships for your highest good.

What is the best way to make these teachings available to children and young adults?

Provide information in a direct, practical manner. There is no need to "talk down" to children or young adults, or to be overly simplistic in endeavors to communicate. Present the facts and let them see their usefulness. For young adults, have good books and other learning aids available. If they are interested in learning, they will learn.

Most important: be a good role model. Let children and everyone with whom you interact be inspired by your God-centered presence, optimistic mental attitude, and wholesome, practical lifestyle.

When I try to help friends and members of my family by sharing some of what I have learned and is helpful to me, what I say is often rejected or not appreciated.

Wait until your advice is requested, then share it as a possibility to be considered and allow others to decide if they want to accept it. Except with children or a person with whom a teacher-student relationship has been established, I never advise or share an opinion.

After having taught these spiritual growth principles for many years, are you satisfied with the results that you have seen?

It is enjoyable to be informed of the benefits that have been experienced by those who have learned and diligently applied these methods. When informed about someone who is not interested in learning, has difficulty in understanding, or who understands but is unwilling or unable to help themselves, although I am compassionate, I am not disappointed. I do what I can do to share useful information and provide support and encouragement. Beyond that, every person has his or her destiny to fulfill in relationship with the Infinite. I trust in the goodness and rightness of life's processes, knowing that the awareness of all souls is certain to be eventually restored to wholeness. I play my role as I understand it to be, and am content to allow the trends of events to be determined by *That* which knows what is best for everyone.

After several years of metaphysical reading, attempts to meditate effectively and live a good life, I am retired from work and I am still confused. I lack self-confidence and my faith in God is weak. What can I do that will make a positive difference in my life?

The only solution to the problem is to decide to be *Self*-confident and to replace thoughts and feelings of fear and doubt with soul-based courage and pure faith. Although you may at times be inspired and encouraged by someone, you are the only person who can make a positive difference in your life.

Avoid thoughts and feelings of despair and morbid preoccupation with your egocentric needs. Don't whine or complain or feel sorry for yourself. Decide what you need to do to make your life worthwhile, and do it!

I sometimes feel what I describe as God's presence. What should I do when I do not have this feeling?

When a vivid sense of awareness of God's presence is lacking, rely on "knowing" that you are in God. You are always in God even when a feeling-awareness of God's presence is not discerned.

I have an intellectual understanding of the enlivening Power that nurtures the universe, me, and everything. What is the best way to cooperate with it?

Improve your understanding of it and its processes and live an orderly, uncomplicated, spiritually directed life. You will then become increasingly aware of God's presence and the supportive inclinations of life.

You, and others I know, started on your spiritual path at an early age. I became interested in spiritual matters much later. It is still possible for me to awaken to Self- and God-realization during my remaining years here?

It is useful to start on a spiritual path at an early age because if what is learned is wisely applied, one's life can be more enjoyable and productive. For you, the important thing is that you are now on the right course in life. Time need not be a factor in regard to spiritual growth. You are, at the innermost level of your being, a flawless unit of God's being. You can awaken to Self- and God-realization quickly by cultivating awareness of what you are and what God is.

Don't be limited by beliefs about the age of your body. Don't associate too much with others who think of themselves as "senior citizens" or whose lives are determined by that belief. Stand firm in the knowledge that you are an immortal, spiritual being and it is your destiny to be fully awake in God. Be happy!

I know with my intellect that I am in God, and often feel that I am, yet my personal circumstances are neither harmonious nor fulfilling. What else can I do?

Examine your mental attitudes and behaviors and discover the relationship between them and what you are experiencing. Control your thinking, emotions, and behaviors and learn to make wise choices. Do what can be done to contribute to harmonious circumstances. Rather than think that you will be fulfilled only when circumstances are as you imagine they should be, cultivate soul-contentment and learn to be fulfilled within yourself. Don't rely on external events and conditions for your peace of mind.

Explain more about God's grace.

The impulses of Consciousness which contribute to our spontaneous spiritual awakenings, provide for our needs, and cause supportive events to occur in timely and appropriate ways are referred to as actions of grace. Grace is expressive without our having to earn its influences or the results of its actions. Its effects are always for our highest good and are more obvious to us when we are receptive to its inclinations. Receptivity to the actions of grace is improved when we are humble, peaceful, and conscious of needing help in our endeavors. We should be thankful for the benefits that the actions of grace freely provide for our well-being.

Impulses of grace enliven the realm of nature, maintain nature's orderly processes, and empower and direct the trends of evolution. Impulses of grace also arise from within us because God's wholeness includes us. When we do our best to live effectively and nurture spiritual awareness, grace becomes increasingly influential in our lives. When we are almost spiritually enlightened, the final awakening is due to God's grace.

A disciple approached the teacher and asked, "I pray that I might be worthy of your good will and God's grace."

The teacher replied, "My good will, and God's grace, you already have. All that is needed is your own acceptance of what is freely available to you."

How can I know if it is God's will that I be spiritually enlightened in my current incarnation?

Your sincere interest in actualizing your potential to be fully awake is an obvious indication that you are being impelled to do it. Explore the possibilities that are now available to you to learn, grow, and become more aware of your innate powers and abilities. As you concentrate your attention and actions on important matters, your spiritual growth will surely be rapid and satisfying. Your right endeavors, and God's grace, will result in complete spiritual fulfillment.

Instead of thinking that God has desires as we do, observe life's inclinations to fulfill higher purposes. The ultimate purpose for which you, and all souls, are in this world is to awaken to Self-knowledge and God-realization. As your ordinary states of awareness are replaced by spiritual awareness, you will have more understanding of these processes and will know God's will (inclination) for you.

Appendix

Understanding the Reality of God

Author's Note:

The information in the appendix is provided as a supplement to the text to emphasize its importance to readers who are intent on comprehending philosophical concepts that will enrich their lives and enable them to progress to higher levels of understanding.

Having accurate knowledge of God allows our spiritual growth to occur more easily. An understanding of the orderly processes of cosmic manifestation enables us to live more effectively.

If some of these concepts are new to you, as you continue to patiently examine them you will have intuitive insights during which aspects of the reality of God and cosmic processes are clearly comprehended. As your innate knowledge is progressively unveiled, you will be able to comprehend the wholeness of God. Nothing will be hidden; you will be spiritually enlightened.

For centuries, philosophers and sages in many parts of the world aspired to discover the truth about the reality of God and how and why the universe came into manifestation. By using their highly developed powers of intelligence and intuition, some of them were able to discern the subtle interactions that occur; the universal laws of causes and their effects; why and how souls manifest and become involved with material realms; and why and how souls awaken from ego-confined states and have their awareness restored to Self- and God-realization.

One Reality (supreme Consciousness) is expressing as the forces and forms of nature. Because knowledge of Consciousness is within it, as units of Consciousness all knowledge of God and nature is within us. What we need to know if we are to function effectively in this or any realm is presently available to us; if it is not yet known it can be discovered.

The Field of Absolute (Pure) Consciousness and the Oversoul (Godhead) Aspect of God

Absolute Consciousness is devoid of characteristics, yet contains limitless possibilities. It makes possible the manifestation of the field of nature while its essential state remains unchanged. We can apprehend pure consciousness during interludes of spontaneous transcendence and learn to be aware of it at will by alert practice of superconscious meditation. While pure consciousness can be intuitively discerned and directly realized, it cannot be described with words that will satisfy the mind or intellect, both of which are material faculties used to apprehend what is thought about or perceived.

The Oversoul aspect of God which blossomed from the field of pure Consciousness has three attributes which can be described and their influences observed.

The three constituent attributes exist because of interactions of polarities in the Oversoul which cause changes and transformations of cosmic forces. They are defined as 1) the power of the positive pole to attract and illuminate; 2) the influence of the negative pole that produces inertia; 3) transformative actions that occur between the power of attraction and inertia. The Sanskrit word for these attributes is *guna* (that which regulates or controls what it influences) and they are named, respectively, 1) *sattwa*, 2) *tamas*, 3) *rajas*.

Pervading the field of nature, the gunas influence the

changes that occur in all realms. Sattwa guna attracts cosmic forces in the field of nature to the Oversoul. Tamas guna causes gross manifestation of cosmic forces. Rajas guna transforms. On the spiritual path, one is advised to 1) resist and overcome tamasic influences (which may contribute to mental dullness and apathy) by engaging in purposeful actions; 2) regulate rajasic influences (which may cause mental and physical restlessness) by nurturing sattwic (pure, elevating) qualities; 3) eventually overcome or rise above all of the influences of the gunas and be Self-directed.

When we experience preliminary superconscious states, tamas guna may contribute to mental dullness; rajas guna may cause mental restlessness or emotional instability that interfere with concentration and elicit perceptions of distracting subjective phenomena. The influence of sattwa guna supports meditation practice.

When the three attributes in the Oversoul are in a balanced state, a universe does not exist. When the equilibrium is disturbed by an impulse that arises in the Oversoul, the gunas again become influential and a universe emerges which may persist for trillions of solar years until it is withdrawn into the Oversoul.

The three attributes in the Oversoul aspect of God permanently prevail. When influences of one attribute are dominant, the other attributes have potential to influence. That is why even the influences of sattwa guna must eventually be transcended by the devotee who is intent on liberation of consciousness.

When soul awareness is supported by sattwa guna,

varying degrees of rajasic and tamasic influences may also be experienced. A devotee may erroneously think, "Now I am established in bliss and have knowledge of Consciousness and its processes; I have attained the final stage of spiritual awakening." Satisfaction with pleasurable meditative states and partial knowledge of God and cosmic processes that results in complacency is an obstacle to further spiritual awakening.

During the early autumn of 1959, I visited my guru at his private retreat in California's Mojave Desert. During our conversation, in response to my inquiry about higher states of consciousness and the means by which they could be realized, he said, "Many saints are content to enjoy the bliss of God-communion and don't aspire to go beyond that stage." After a brief pause, he said, "You must go all the way!"

When we direct our attention inward to experience our true nature, we can discern the reality of God and have our faith nurtured as we continue to engage in spiritual practices that will enable us to awaken to liberation of consciousness.

Objective manifestation of cosmic forces begins when the power of Consciousness is projected from the Oversoul aspect of God. As you read these descriptions of the twenty-four categories of cosmic manifestation, remember that, at the innermost level of your being, you already know these principles and processes.

The Field of Primordial Nature

The projected power of Consciousness produces a

vibration (Om) within which space, time, and cosmic forces are produced. A universe is formed by the interactions of cosmic forces which manifest as fine particles and atoms. We ordinarily see only a few wavelengths of the electromagnetic field that pervades space. Radio frequencies, gamma rays, microwaves, X-rays, and other frequencies can be discerned by using special instruments.

The Sanskrit word for this first field of nature is *maya*, from the verb-root *ma*, "to measure." It is said to be truth-veiling because identification of our attention and awareness with its characteristics can weaken our powers of perception. It is the womb of creation that gives birth to the universe, which is why in some religious traditions it is thought of as a divine mother, a feminine form-producing aspect of God.

When the awareness of souls is blurred, they do not perceive the inner side of life. They may observe objective effects but not their hidden causes. Insightful metaphysical studies and spiritual practices can enable us to perceive and comprehend the fine essences and attributes which may not otherwise be easily discerned.

The universe is not an illusion: it exists, and can be observed, examined, defined, and described. One who examines the external characteristics of nature without comprehending its inner aspects is liable to mistakenly presume the impermanent to be permanent and be inclined to believe the material universe to be the only reality. An inability to know what is true can result in delusions.

When born into the material world, the soul may be

so identified with it and its processes that the ability to apprehend the fine aspects which produced and maintains the world is diminished. Thus sense-bound, the soul is in need of awakening from material consciousness to spiritual awareness. Unless an ego- and sense-confined soul awakens and actualizes its spiritual potential, it cannot fully comprehend the true nature of the universe or the reality of God.

Simplistic explanations for the purpose of world manifestation have been offered from time to time to pacify unenlightened minds. One childish story is: "Because God was lonely, he created the worlds and souls to have companionship and enjoyment." Another equally false opinion is that God created the worlds to provide souls an opportunity to choose a relationship with him or to deny him and be punished. Such ideas reveal the spiritual ignorance of those who profess to believe them.

Fluctuations of the gunas in the Oversoul start the process of world manifestation. A universe can be said to be of value because it allows life to flourish and provides opportunities for souls to express as they awaken from egocentric states of consciousness to God-realization.

Although only spiritual enlightenment can liberate us, it can be useful to engage in intellectual analysis of God and the universe if such inquiry clarifies our awareness and results in higher understanding that enables us to live effectively. It is not useful, however, to be preoccupied with superficial metaphysical speculation.

When the primordial field from which gross matter emerges is expressive, sattwa guna produces a celestial realm where souls which are not yet involved with gross matter, and those awakening from it, abide. This realm is not the final destination. There, souls may continue to awaken to Self-knowledge or may again become involved with gross matter in accord with their inclinations and the influences of the gunas on their mental states and states of consciousness.

Categories #1 – 4
Objective Cosmic Individualization
(Self-Sense, Ego, Mind, and Intellect)

At this stage, the influence of tamas guna modifies Consciousness. The influence of rajas guna produces a Universal Mind in which cosmic actions are coordinated. Just as influences of the constituent attributes of nature modify the one Consciousness as it expresses in the direction of objective manifestation, they modify the awareness of souls that are involved with cosmic processes. The unit (Self) then becomes aware of being an individualized part of the whole. The influence of tamas guna contracts soul awareness and contributes to an illusional sense of self (ego). The influence of rajas guna produces the mind used by the ego-confined soul. The influences of sattwa guna produce the faculty of intellect. It should be noted that mental and intellectual faculties are not attributes of the soul; they are used by the soul when relating to objective phenomena. Higher realities are intuitively discerned and directly experienced. That is why thinking about and intellectually analyzing the reality of God can only result in partial understanding.

When individualized units of pure consciousness are expressed because of a mixing of influences of the Oversoul and its projected power, they become aware of a sense of Self-identity. When their awareness is modified by the influences of the gunas, they assume an illusional sense of self-identity (ego-consciousness), assume mental and intellectual faculties, and are liable to incarnate in causal, astral, or physical realms. Before their awareness is modified by the gunas, being Self-aware and Self-knowing, they are conscious of their relationship with God.

Categories #5 – 24
The Capacities of Sense Perception,
Actions, and Objective Manifestation
of Cosmic Forces

The forces of attraction and repulsion manifest a magnetic field with five electric radiations that produce a causal (capable of causing effects) field from which gross matters are emanated. The electric radiations are manifested with the influences of the gunas: two from the extremities, the positive and negative poles (sattwa and tamas); one from the middle (rajas); and two from the gaps between them. The characteristics produced between the gaps are a blend of sattwa-rajas and rajas-tamas.

- *The Five Senses*. The sense capacities that enable us to have touch sensation, and to smell, taste, hear, and see are produced by the influence of sattwa guna. Sensory input is received by the mind and presented to the intellect for interpretation. Because the mind is the seat of sense perceptions, we can experience vivid perceptions and sensations when dreaming and when memories influence the mind and emotions while we are awake.

- *The Capacities to Perform Actions.* The neutralizing attributes of the five radiations influenced by rajas guna produce the capacities for speech, mobility in space, manual dexterity, elimination, and reproduction. The seat of these five capacities is the astral or life force covering of the soul.

  The five sense capacities and five capacities that enable the performance of actions, along with the mind and intellect, comprise the fine causal body which a soul uses in gross or subtle realms. The causal body may be transcended when the soul awakens to full God-realization and karmic conditions and inclinations to relate to relative realms no longer prevail.

- *Element-Influences and Objects of Perception.* The influences of tamas guna cause the production of five subtle essences (with their influences) of gross elements which can then manifest as a physical universe which is perceived through the five senses and enable souls to have material desires satisfied.

The five subtle element-essences and their influences which manifest a universe are described as ether, air, fire, water, and earth. *Ether* is a term used for space with cosmic forces. The element-influences, regulated by the three gunas, determine the basic constitution of life forms and their functions. From this knowledge *Ayurveda* ("life-knowledge") evolved: a holistic system of well-being based on balancing element-influences or governing principles of the mind and body. When the mind-body constitution is balanced, radiant health, psychological wellness, and mental clarity prevails.

The five subtle capacities of perception, five subtle capacities of action, five subtle element-essences, five gross elements, the mind, the faculty of intelligence, the sense of individual Self-awareness, and ego-sense comprise the twenty-four aspects of cosmic manifestation. The entire cosmic body includes God as the Oversoul and all of the manifestations of its attributes expressing in and as the field of nature. As cosmic processes are directed from the field of God, so our mental and physical processes can be directed from soul awareness. We can learn about the reality of the universe and God by turning within and learning about the forces and attributes used by the soul while we are involved in the physical realm. By knowing our true nature and the processes of life we can know God and the categories and processes of the cosmos.

The Seven Realms of Cosmic Manifestation

Seven realms provide the fields of operations of cosmic processes. From the negative pole of the field of primordial nature, a force is repulsed that emanates the worlds. From the positive pole of primordial nature the power of attraction keeps creation in balance and eventually redeems it by attracting the forces of nature back to their source. The inertia of the primordial field partially obscures divine qualities; its prevailing power of attraction unveils them. Tamasic influences produce gross nature; the transformative influences of rajas guna maintain it. The purifying influence of sattwa guna enables living things to be capable of expressing their innate divine qualities.

The Seven Realms

1. *The Oversoul.* Souls that awaken to this realm may remain in it if they are fully enlightened or become involved with gross realms if tamas guna is influential. If rajas guna influences prevail, the soul perceives and experiences what occurs in the realm of the Oversoul. When sattwa guna influences prevail, the soul may transcend the influences of the gunas and experience pure existence-bliss.

2. *Realm of the Spirit of God.* Manifested when the impulse to express becomes influential. The Spirit of God is the enlivening influence that moves in the direction of manifestation and regulates cosmic processes.

3. *Realm of Spiritual Reflection.* Produced when rays of God shine on, and are reflected by, the field of primordial nature. Here, Cosmic Individuality occurs and units of pure consciousness are individualized. Illumined souls may also reside here.

4. *Primordial Nature.* Om, with its attributes of space, time, and cosmic forces. This realm and the realm of spiritual reflection are dual aspects of the emanated creative force. They mix to further the manifesting process.

5. *Causal Realm.* Subtle faculties of the five capacities of sense perception, the five capacities which enable action, and five element-essences are expressed to make possible further projections of cosmic forces.

6. *Astral Realm.* Astral bodies of souls are nourished by vital forces that flow through the chakras and the subtle channels which extend from them.

7. *Realm of Gross Matter.* The physical universe. In the physical body, seven astral centers (chakras) through which life forces flow are located in the spine and brain. A meditator can internalize attention by moving awareness upwards through the chakras. This is a practical way to meditate effectively and acquire direct knowledge of the seven realms of cosmic manifestation.

Souls that relate to fine and gross levels of matter express through five sheaths (coverings):

1. *Bliss Sheath.* Thus named because when clarified awareness is identified with only a fine covering of consciousness-as-matter, it experiences superior well-being and pure joy of Self-awareness. Since this is not yet the ultimate state to be realized, it will eventually be transcended.

2. *Intellect Sheath.* Which enables an embodied soul to use powers of discrimination to acquire knowledge.

3. *Mental Sheath.* With mental faculties and capacities that process perceptions, thoughts, and memories.

4. *Life Force Sheath.* The astral body nourished by the soul's life force (prana).

5. *Physical Sheath.* The body nourished by food.

A universe is manifested as fine, gaseous, fiery, liquid, and solid matters. From a singularity, a source-point without dimensions, a universe emerges. The energy to be expressive in and as a universe is present in this original source-point. The total quantity of energy of a universe neither increases nor decreases; it is only transformed. Gross matter is confined energy.

When conditions on a planet are suitable for the emergence of consciousness, God's power of attraction unveils life forces, freeing them to express. When the cosmic sheath with capacities to perform actions is unveiled, the vegetable kingdom emerges. When the cosmic sheath with capacities of sense perception is unveiled, simple organisms and higher life forms are evolved. When the cosmic sheath of intellect is unveiled, humankind emerges. When the innermost sheath is unveiled, the innate capacities and knowledge of souls unfold. When the fine sheath of consciousness-as-matter is transcended, souls complete their awakening to full enlightenment.

The three attributes of nature may influence our mental attitudes and personal behaviors:

- When sattwic influences prevail, we are inclined to be cheerful, optimistic, energetic, kind, honest, self-disciplined, creatively purposeful, and to adhere to healthy lifestyle regimens and spiritual practices.
- When rajasic influences prevail, we may be inclined to be restless, experience fluctuations in moods and men-

tal states, be undisciplined in our behaviors, and be attracted or addicted to sensual enjoyment.

• Tamasic influences may incline us to be apathetic, physically sluggish, intellectually lazy, and to prefer relationships and behaviors which may be useless, harmful, or destructive.

Choose wholesome lifestyle regimens that enhance all aspects of your life and support your aspiration to satisfy your innate desire to know God. Cultivate and actualize your sattwic (pure, elevating) attributes.

While being intentional on our spiritual path, it is essential that we maintain our integrity in regard to our relationships with others and our environment. We can do this by always being outwardly appropriate while inwardly unwavering in our commitment to Self- and God-realization. Our lifestyle should enable us to fulfill our obligations while we continue our spiritual practices and awaken to higher states of consciousness.

When your intelligence ... is firm in realization of oneness, then shall you awaken to flawless Self-knowledge.

— Bhagavad Gita 2:53

Glossary

Glossary

Words and Concepts to Know

absolute Perfect, complete. Pure, not mixed. Not limited.

action The process of doing.

actualize To realize in action. Abilities are actualized when they are expressed. Goals are actualized when they are accomplished.

affirm Latin *affirmāre*, to strengthen. To declare to be true. Affirmations can help to clarify our thinking, harmonize our emotions, and adjust our states of consciousness. The key to using affirmations effectively is to emphatically declare what is desired to be true as though it were real until conscious realization of what is affirmed is actualized.

agnosticism The theory that asserts that God cannot be known, that only sense-perceived phenomena are objects of exact knowledge.

alienation Isolation; a sense of removal or separation.

apathy Lack of (emotional) feeling. Disinterest. A major obstacle to higher learning that should be replaced by a strong will-to-live and to accomplish meaningful purposes.

astral The field or realm of life forces, and its phenomena.

atheism Disbelief of the existence of God.

attention Alert observation: concentration.

avatar The emergence of divine qualities and powers in human form. In some religious traditions: a spiritually enlightened soul that incarnates for the purpose of infusing divine influences into planetary consciousness. The "universal avatar" concept is that divine qualities become increasingly influential as individual and collective consciousness becomes illumined.

awareness A state of being conscious of something. We can even be aware of being aware.

ayurveda Sanskrit *ayus*, life, and *veda*, knowledge. A natural way to nurture total well-being that evolved in India several centuries ago. Diagnostic procedures include examination of the patient's pulse, temperature, skin condition, eyes, behavior, and psychological characteristics.

Procedures used to restore and maintain balance of the basic mind-body constitution may include the use of foods and herbs, attitude adjustment, behavior modification, massage and other body work, meditation practice, and detoxification of the body.

belief The act, condition, or habit of having trust or confidence in a person, thing, or idea, especially the opinions or doctrines firmly believed by a group of persons.

Bhagavad Gita Holy or divine song, from *bhaj*, to revere or love, and *gai*, song. An allegoric literary work in which Krishna (representing enlightened consciousness) is portrayed as an avatar teaching his disciple-friend Arjuna "the eternal way of righteousness" with emphasis on knowledge, selfless service, devotion, and meditation.

bliss Spiritual bliss is the joy of awareness of pure being rather than a pleasant emotion or feeling.

brain The main part of the central nervous system that processes sensory impulses, thoughts, and emotions, and coordinates and regulates bodily activities.

capacity The ability to receive, hold, absorb, learn, or do. When our capacity to experience the reality of God is increased, we are able to apprehend and know it. At the core of our being, we already know our relationship with God. Our capacity to experience the reality of God can be increased by purifying the mind and nurturing superconscious awareness.

causal realm The field of cosmic, electrical, and magnetic forces emanated from the field of primordial nature that further express as astral and physical realms.

chakra Sanskrit "wheel." Any of the seven vital centers in the spine and brain, with unique attributes.
  The first chakra at the base of the spine has the earth element attribute. The prana frequency taste is sweet; the color is yellow; the sound is as restless buzzing of bees. Sanskrit *muladhara*, "foundation." A characteristic of this chakra is stability.
  Second chakra: At the sacrum of the spine. Water element. The taste is astringent; the color is white; the sound is like that of a flute. Sanskrit *swadhisthana*, "abode of self-consciousness." A characteristic influence is sensuality.
  Third chakra: At the lumbar region of the spine opposite the navel. Fire element. The taste is bitter; the color is red; the sound is like that of a harp. Sanskrit *manipura*, "the city of jewels." When awareness is identified here, one may express self-control and fervent aspiration to spiritual growth.
  Fourth chakra: At the dorsal region of the spine between the shoulder blades. Air element. The taste is sour; the color is blue; the sound is like a continuous peal of a gong. Sanskrit *anahata*, "unstruck sound." When awareness is identi-

fied here, one may have mastery of the senses and life forces.

Fifth Chakra: At the cervical region of the spine, opposite the throat. Ether (space) element. The taste is pungent; the color is gray or misty with sparkling pinpoints of white light; the sound is like the roar of the ocean. Sanskrit *vishudda*, "pure." When awareness is identified here, one may have exceptional powers of intellectual and intuitive discernment.

Sixth Chakra: Between the eyebrows, associated with the front lobes of the brain. Life forces flowing upward and focused here may be perceived as a dark blue orb with a golden halo centered with a silver-white light. Gold is said to be the life force frequency of Om; dark blue, the frequency of all-pervading Consciousness; the white starlike light has all of the colors of light wavelengths. Sanskrit *ajna*, "command."

Seventh Chakra: Related, but not confined, to the higher brain. Pure consciousness, transcendence of mental and physical states and of all conditions that modify or distort awareness. Sanskrit *sahasrara*, "thousand rayed."

channeling A modern word for mediumship: the belief that souls which have departed from this world can be contacted by telepathic or other means for the purpose of communication. Some people at the second stage of soul unfoldment try to contact souls in astral realms to prove that life continues after physical death or to acquire "higher" knowledge. Their endeavors would be more spiritually useful if they concentrated on actualizing their own divine qualities. Anyone who claims to communicate in this manner is either self-deceived or dishonest. Sincere truth seekers should not indulge in such activities, nor should they associate with persons who do.

chant A simple, melodic lyric repeatedly intoned or sung. Studies have indicated that chanting reduces stress, calms the mind, and contributes to balanced interactions between the left and right hemispheres of the brain.

character The combined mental, emotional, and moral qualities of a person. A distinguishing feature or attribute.

compassion Empathetic concern for the suffering or misfortune of others, or for social or environmental conditions that need to be nurtured, together with an inclination to provide aid or support.

concentration An undisturbed flow of attention.

conscience The faculty of recognizing the difference between what is right and wrong in regard to one's conduct along with a sense that one should act accordingly. Compliant conformity to one's sense of proper conduct.

consciousness In ordinary usage: a state of being aware. Also, the totality of attitudes and opinions held or thought to be held by a group or an individual. When spelled with an upper case C, it is used to refer to God or supreme Reality.

contemplate Latin *com*, intensive; *templum*, space for observing a sign or indication. To ponder or to consider as being possible. To hopefully look at or observe with keen expectation of discovery. Contemplation, when meditating, involves concentration on a chosen object with which one desires to identify or a concept about which knowledge is desired.

cosmic consciousness Awareness of the unified wholeness of life. As we become more spiritually aware, cosmic conscious insights become more frequent.

decisive Characterized by determined or resolute choice.

deduction To arrive at a conclusion by disregarding what is not valid. When what cannot be true is removed, what remains is true.

deism The belief that God created the universe, but is apart from it, has no influence on phenomena, and provides no revelation.

delusion An erroneous idea or belief.

deserve To be worthy of having.

desire To wish for or want. Desires enable us to achieve goals or accomplish purposes. Life-enhancing desires that contribute to our well-being are acceptable. Obsessive cravings that disturb the mind, interfere with rational thinking, cause emotional unrest, and impel unwise or erratic behaviors should be avoided, renounced, or replaced by wholesome, life-enhancing desires.

devotion Attachment or loyalty to something or someone. Devotion to God purifies the mind and enables us to identify with God. The resolve of one who is devoted to the spiritual path does not waver.

dharma That which upholds, supports, or maintains. When we live constructively with a clear sense of purpose that is of value to us, others, and the environment, we have the full support of the forces and resources of nature.

diligent Careful, attentive, persevering.

disciple Latin *discipulus*, learner or student. On a spiritual path: an adherent of a philosophical system or spiritual tradition.

effect An event, condition, or circumstance produced by a cause.

effective Having or producing a desired result. The capacity to live effectively enables us to accomplish our purposes.

ego Common definition: the sense of self as distinct from one's environment. The aspect that relates to external reality and directs behaviors. *Metaphysical*: an illusional (mistaken) sense of selfhood that causes and sustains a false sense of self-identity. When the ego is purified, we are aware of being an individualized unit of infinite Consciousness.

egotism An exaggerated or extreme sense of self importance, often characterized by arrogance, self-centered mental attitudes, and selfish or controlling personal behaviors.

elicit To bring forth. Deep physical relaxation is elicited when we meditate correctly. Superconscious states are elicited when the mind is calm and emotions are quieted.

emotion A subjective feeling-response to something: compassion, love (attraction), aversion, fear, revulsion, elation, or any other feeling-response that one might have.

emotional maturity The state or quality of having reached our full growth in regard to being able to easily regulate thinking and mental and emotional impulses and to realistically and appropriately relate to our environment and other people. A functional degree of emotional maturity is necessary if authentic spiritual growth is to be experienced.

enlightenment To provide with knowledge. When we have accurate knowledge of mundane matters, we are enlightened in regard to them. When we are spiritually enlightened, we have knowledge of our true nature and the reality of God. It should not be presumed that a spiritually enlightened person knows everything about us or the relative world in which we live, nor should it be thought that he or she has no "human" characteristics. When spiritually enlightened, one may still have karmic conditions to overcome or tendencies that need to be controlled.

era A duration of time. Centuries ago, sages in India estimated recurring time-cycles in accord with astronomical calculations. They divided a 24,000 year cycle into four subcycles: a Dark Age duration of 1,200 years during which confusion and spiritual ignorance prevails on the planet; 2,400 years during which the collective consciousness partially awakens, some people become aware of the existence of nature's finer forces (electricity and magnetism), and technological and scientific discoveries occur; 3,600 years during which more people on the planet become aware of their mental and spiritual capacities; 4,800 years of an Age of widespread spiritual enlightenment. According to this theory, we are now a little over 300 years into an ascending 2,400 year cycle, which conditions in our current era seem to validate.

Many people who are not aware of this theory of cosmic cycles, or who prefer to maintain their traditional opinions, say that we are in a Kali Yuga (*kali*, spiritual darkness and confusion; *yuga*, era). They may think this to be so because, since we are only 300 years removed from the last Dark Age, some characteristics of that era have not yet receded.

evolution A gradual, transformative process during which something changes, usually to a better form or condition.

faith Confident belief in the truth, value, or reliability of an idea, person, or thing.

field An area or space in which events occur. The Oversoul aspect of supreme Consciousness, Universal Mind, the realm of primordial nature, and the causal, astral, and physical realms are fields, as is our awareness. Physics: a region of space indicated by physical properties such as gravity and weak and strong electromagnetic forces.

God The one Reality. The absolute aspect is existence-being.

The expressive aspect has attributes which pervade it and its emanated power (Om).

good fortune Circumstances that provide comfort, satisfaction, and prosperity.

grace Freely given benefits, good fortune, or support. What we refer to as God's grace are 1) the impulses that empower evolution and nurture and sustain it, the universe, and all living things; 2) the influence of attraction from the Oversoul that awakens our innate powers and contributes to our well-being and spiritual growth. Although the effects of grace in our lives are more evident when we are receptive to them, they are influential even when we are not aware of them. When we have done all that we know to do to assist ourselves to Self- and God-realization, grace is influential in liberating our consciousness.

guna A constituent attribute of Consciousness pervading it and nature that regulates cosmic forces. Three in number, their influences are described as being *sattwic*, illuminating; *rajasic*, transformative; *tamasic*, inertial.

guru That which removes darkness. A teacher. In enlightenment traditions, a guru is viewed as a person through whom spiritual knowledge and transformative influences can be transmitted to receptive persons.

hallucination A false or distorted perception of objects or events with a strong sense of their reality. Subjective, mind-brain produced phenomena.

heart Metaphysical meaning: the essence of one's being. When a spiritual teacher advises a disciple to "seek out the truth in his or her heart" it should be understood that their true nature is to be contemplated and realized.

heal To make whole. To restore to complete health, wellness, or spiritual wholeness.

holistic Emphasis on the whole (totality) and the interdependence of its parts. Holistic living requires the harmonious integration of all aspects of our lives. The aim of a holistic approach to healing is to effect a harmonious balance of the spiritual, mental, emotional, physical, and environmental components of the patient's life.

holy Of divine character or origin.

humility Absence of egotism. Compliant acknowledgment of our true nature in relationship with God. For a truth seeker, humility is an essential quality to nurture. For a spiritually enlightened person, humility is a natural characteristic.

illusion Latin *illūsiō*, an imitation. A flawed perception of subjective or objective reality—of thoughts, concepts, feelings, or external things or events.

imagination A mental picture or concept of something which does not yet exist or does not exist in the present environment. Fantasy is unregulated imagination. Controlled imagining causes (or allows) desires to be fulfilled.

infer "To bring in." To determine the solution of a problem or the outcome of events based on knowledge of premises or evidence.

initiation A "new beginning." Many life-enhancing experiences or events are initiations. In some enlightenment traditions, formal initiation is an occasion of acceptance into the company of adherents of specific teachings and personal instruction in spiritual practices and lifestyle regimens is given.

inspired Latin *inspīrāre*: *in-*, into, and *spīrāre*, to breath. To be aroused, affected, or guided by divine influence.

intellect The faculty of discrimination or discernment. Intellectual inquiry can enable us to acquire a conceptual understanding of the reality of God. Beyond that stage, intuition can provide direct insight.

intention Latin intentĭō, attention, from *intendĕre*, to intend (to do something). An aim, plan, or purpose to be actualized. A truth seeker's thoughts and actions should be intentional.

intensive Done with deliberate, concentrated, purposeful endeavor. Spiritual practice should be intensive.

intuition Direct perception without the aid of the senses.

karma An influence that can cause effects to occur. Accumulated mental conditionings and influential subliminal tendencies and urges comprise one's personal karmic condition (which is of the mind and body, not of the soul).

kundalini Soul force. In people who are not spiritually awake, it is mostly dormant. In spiritually awake people, its energies are active, transformative, and empowering. Its energies are aroused by aspiration to spiritual growth, devotion, meditation and other practices, being in places where spiritual forces are strong, and mental and spiritual attunement with an enlightened person.

life The quality of living things manifested in functions such as growth, metabolism, response to stimuli, and reproduction. Also the physical, mental, and spiritual experiences that make up our sense of existence.

light Electromagnetic radiation. Light travels at 186,000 miles per second. The sun's radiation travels 93 million miles in almost 8 minutes to our planet where we perceive some of it as visible light when it impacts earth's magnetic field. We can be affected by light (or its absence). For health purposes, regular exposure to daylight (without wearing glasses) is recommended. In regions of the world where the winter season is long or sunlight is minimal, some people experience episodes of mental depression because of lack of sunlight. In such instances, supplemental exposure to bright, electric powered light is recommended. Light can also cause changes in liquid foods such as honey, milk, and fruit and vegetable juices. For this reason it is recommended that these liquids be stored in light proof containers or in a cupboard.

love Intense affection (fondness) for something or someone.

mantra From Sanskrit *manas*, mind; and *tra*, to protect. A word, word-phrase, or sound used to focus attention.

mastery Having command over something. Self-mastery is accomplished when states of awareness, thoughts, emotions, and behaviors are easily controlled.

material A substance of which something is made.

matter Something that occupies space. Formed matter is energy confined in a small space. It has been suggested that 95 percent of the matter in the universe (named "dark matter") pervades space and is invisible. Its existence is inferred by its influences which can be detected and calculated.

meaningful Having a useful purpose or being of value.

meditation An undisturbed flow of attention to an object or ideal to be identified with or realized. Intentional detachment of attention and awareness from external conditions, the senses, emotions, and mental states that enables one to realize the pure-conscious essence of being and the reality of God.

metaphysics Latin *metaphysica* < Greek *tà metà tà physiká*, the things after the physics, the title of Aristotle's treatise on first principles, so-called because it followed his work on physics. The branch of philosophy that investigates the nature of first principles of ultimate reality, including the study of the nature and attributes of being and cosmology.

mind The faculty used to process perceptions and information.

modify To change the characteristics or condition of something. To limit or restrict. Our ordinary awareness is modified by acquired information, erroneous opinions (delusions), misperceptions of facts (illusion), sleep, and memories. Pure awareness of being, transcendent superconsciousness, is unmodified.

mysticism Spiritual discipline practiced to experience unification of awareness with God or ultimate reality, usually by contemplative meditation. The experience of such realization. Belief in the existence of realities beyond ordinary powers of perception which are accessible by subjective experience, as by intuition.

New Thought A modern religious movement that for more than one hundred years has emphasized the possibility of spiritual healing and the value of positive thinking. Some prominent New Thought organizations are Unity School of Practical Christianity, Science of Mind and its Religious Science churches, and Divine Science. Many of these organizations, and independent movements which promote similar views, are affiliated with the International New Thought Alliance which sponsors annual conferences in major cities.

Om The vibration of the power of Consciousness. In some religious traditions Om is referred to as God's Word (Greek *logos*).

omnipotence Unlimited power.

omnipresence Present everywhere.

omniscience All knowing.

Oversoul The Godhead aspect of supreme Consciousness. The first self-manifested aspect with constituent attributes which emanate or express along with its vibrating power (Om) that produces and sustains a universe.

patience The capacity to calmly persevere in the face of adversity or while waiting for anticipated events to occur.

positive Marked or exhibiting certainty, acceptance, affirmation, or absence of doubt.

possibility Capable of existing, happening, or being true without contradicting known or proven facts, circumstances, or natural laws of cause and effect. Inspired possibility-thinking enables us to imagine events, conditions, and circumstances that we want to experience or have actualized.

prana Life force that sustains and animates living things.

pranayama Sanskrit *pran(a)*, life force; *ayama*, not restrained. The formal practice of pranayama usually involves regulation of breathing rhythms to harmonize flows of life force in the body and calm the mind as preparation for meditation practice.

prayer Latin *prēcaria*, to obtain by entreaty or earnest request. The act of making such a request. A form of communion with God.

primal or **primordial** Happening first in time or sequence: original. The first relative field of cosmic manifestation produced by Om and its unified aspects of space, time, and cosmic forces.

prosperity Thriving. We are truly prosperous when the spiritual, mental, emotional, physical, and environmental components of our lives are harmoniously integrated.

psyche In Western cultures the psyche (Latin from Greek *psykhe*, soul) is usually viewed as the mind functioning as the center of thought, feeling, and behavior and consciously or unconsciously adjusting and relating the body to its social and physical environment.

The practical means by which obstacles to spiritual growth can be removed are the same and can be used by everyone. When first learning about spiritual practices that evolved in other regions of the world, some people have difficulty grasping new philosophical concepts or the words used to describe them. Or they may falsely presume that cultural behaviors unlike their own must be adopted. Acquired mental attitudes and habits may also be a problem: in cultures where self-reliance and a strong sense of individualism is emphasized, resistance to having a teacher or to purifying the ego may be obstacles to learning and spiritual growth.

psychic Of or related to the soul. Natural soul powers of perception and abilities which are commonly considered to be exceptional or extraordinary. Psychic powers may emerge spontaneously along with authentic spiritual growth. They should be used only for constructive purposes.

psychological Of, related to, or derived from the spiritual essence of a person and the mind and emotions.

rational Consistent with reason. Rational thinking is disciplined, orderly examination or analysis of available facts.

realization Direct perception and personal experience. We are Self-realized when we are consciously established in Self-knowledge. We are God-realized when we are consciously established in God-awareness and knowledge.

redemptive The capacity to restore, rescue, free, or liberate. Rightly performed spiritual practices, and God's grace, are redemptive.

reincarnation The return of souls to physical embodiment because of necessity or the soul's inclination to have experiences here. It is not spiritually beneficial to be overly concerned about possible previous or future earth sojourns. Our attention and endeavors should be focused on authentic spiritual growth that will result in liberation of consciousness.

sacred Latin *sacer*, "dedicated or consecrated to a divinity or to something considered to be holy."

sage A wise person.

salvation Liberation from pain or discomfort, which may be temporary or permanent in accord with one's degree of Self- and God-realization. Liberation of consciousness.

samadhi Oneness, wholeness. Superconsciousness that prevails when our awareness is removed from or is no longer influenced by mental or emotional states. Preliminary meditative samadhi is usually supported by an object of perception. Transcendent meditative states are devoid of supporting objects. The final stage of superconsciousness is accomplished when we are fully awake (spiritually enlightened) at all times, regardless of whether we are meditating or engaged in activities and relationships.

Sanatana Dharma The eternal righteous (right) way, commonly referred to as Hinduism. The timeless philosophical system that emphasizes constructive, wholesome living and spiritual practice that enables us to be in harmony with the orderly processes of nature and to know our relationship with God.

The Sindhu river forming part of the western boundary of India was referred to by ancient Persians as the *Hindu* river. The Greeks changed the name to *Indos*, which was later converted into English as *Indus*. The Greeks referred to the country east of the "Indos" as India. Its inhabitants then became known as Hindus and their religious and cultural practices as Hinduism.

science Orderly, disciplined observation, identification, description, and experimental investigation of mundane phenomena or of higher realities.

seer A person who discerns the truth of what is observed.

Self An individualized unit of pure consciousness. Our true nature, rather than the illusional sense of selfhood (ordinary self-consciousness). When identified with matter and a mind and body, the Self is referred to as a soul. Units of pure consciousness are individualized when interactions between the spirit or life of God and primordial nature enable the inertial attribute of Consciousness to be influential. Self-realization occurs when the difference between the essence of being and ordinary awareness is discerned.

shakti Kundalini (soul force) energies that flow when obstructions to their actions are removed. Their awakening and activation can occur spontaneously, as a result of fervent devotion and spiritual practice, and proximity and mental and spiritual attunement with someone in whom they are dynamically active. See *kundalini*.

soul An individualized unit of pure consciousness identified with the illusional sense of selfhood. See *Self.*

space The infinite extension of three-dimensional reality in which events occur.

spirit Latin *spīritus*, breath, from *spīrāre*, to breath. The vital force or principle in living things. The word is sometimes used to refer to a soul, or to the presence of God. The (holy) spirit of God is the vital (animating) essence of God.

spiritual Of or related to God and souls.

stage A level, degree, or period of time in the course of a process.

subjective Produced or existing in the mind or awareness.

subliminal Below the threshold of conscious awareness. Subliminal drives and tendencies activate thoughts and emotions. When they are pacified, the mind is calm and awareness is clear.

superconscious Latin *super*, above or over. Superconscious states are superior to ordinary states of consciousness.

technique A systematic procedure. A meditation *technique* can elicit relaxation, calm the mind, and focus attention.

time An interval between events. Part of a continuum (wholeness) which includes space and cosmic forces, no part of which can be distinguished from the others except by arbitrary (individual judgment) division for the purpose of analysis or for theoretical speculation.

Our concept of time is related to things and events: pendulums swing; quartz crystals vibrate; atoms, light waves, electric and magnetic fields and planets move.

The interval of time we refer to as a solar year marks one orbit of the earth around the sun; a day is one turn of the earth on its axis; a month was once related to the duration of the orbit of the moon. Astronomical measures of time are not absolute; they are constantly changing. The moon is now farther from earth than it was thousands of years ago. Five hundred million years ago, a day was about twenty hours long. Days and years are variable rather than exact markings of time. Our seven-day week is arbitrary. Through the ages, some cultures have had five, eight, and ten day weeks.

Until the fourteenth century, days were divided into irregular intervals of morning, noon, evening, and night. Summer daylight hours are longer than winter daylight hours. Hours and minutes and time zones began to be standardized only a few centuries ago, so that train and other schedules related to distance could be determined.

At the Equator, the earth's rate of spin is 1,000 miles an hour; its speed around the sun is almost 20 miles a second (72,000 miles an hour; 1,728,000 miles each day. Our solar system, in relationship to the center of our galaxy, is moving at the rate of 120 miles a second (432,000 miles an hour). Our galaxy is moving toward another galaxy (Andromeda) at 50 miles a second (180,000 miles an hour).

Time should not be thought of as an insurmountable obstacle to spiritual growth: which can be slow, faster, or rapid in accord with our capacity to learn and awaken, and our intensity of endeavor.

transcendental Rising above common thought, ideas, or stages of consciousness. Interest in the underlying basis of knowledge.

Transcendental Field Absolute or pure Consciousness. Defined as Existence-Being because it does not have attributes. The ultimate stage of spiritual growth to be realized.

transcendentalism The belief or understanding that knowledge of reality is intuitively perceived rather than only by examination of objective experience.

Universal Mind The cosmic mind of which particularized minds are units or parts. Our mental states, subliminal tendencies and urges, thoughts, desires, and intentions interact with Universal Mind which is inclined to respond by manifesting corresponding circumstances.

valid Well-grounded or based on facts. That which produces desired results. Accurate knowledge rationally deduced or inferred from a known premise or available evidence.

virtual From Latin *virtūs*, excellence. Existing in essence if not yet in actual fact or form.

will power The ability and strength of personal resolve to actualize decisions, desires, and plans. Will power should be soul-inspired and impelled rather than ego-motivated.

worthwhile Of sufficient value to justify the application or use of skills, energies, or other resources.

wisdom Understanding of what is true, right, or enduring.

yoga To "yoke" together or "unify." 1. Awareness of being unified with one field of Consciousness. 2. Samadhi (oneness), used in Patanjali's yoga-sutras. 3. The systems used to accomplish Self- and God-realization. Although its practices are based on philosophical concepts, Yoga is not classified as a religion. Yoga practices are believed to have originated in India five thousand or more years ago.

Hatha Yoga practices include asanas (postures) that strengthen muscles, improve flexibility and blood and lymph circulation; mudras (procedures used to acquire a degree of conscious control over involuntary physical functions and awaken kundalini energies); pranayama; and meditation practices.

The Hatha Yoga Pradipika compiled by Yogi Swatmarama (circa 14th century) is a basic text on the subject. In it, unique procedures are integrated with the practices of Raja Yoga as described in chapter two of Patanjali's yoga-sutras. The Sanskrit word *pradipika* can be translated as "light," "self-illuminating," and "that which illumines."

The aim of the dedicated Hatha Yoga practitioner is to cleanse the body, make it immune to disease, and rid it of the limitations that are common to the ordinary person's experience. Hatha Yoga practice removes dullness (tamasic influences) and impurities and balances the mind-body constitution. Complete practice results in the actualization of exceptional abilities and powers of concentration that can be used to effectively practice meditation. The author of *Hatha Yoga Pradipika* asserted, "There are those who only perform Hatha Yoga without knowledge of Raja Yoga; them I consider to be deprived of the fruit (results) of their endeavors. If prana (life force) does not flow in the middle passage [subtle channel in the spine], if the source-essence of life force is not steadied by regulated prana, if the mind does not reflect [the results of] spontaneous meditation, those who [claim to] speak of spiritual knowledge are only indulging in boastful, false assertions."

Bhakti Yoga: the way of love, compassion, devotion to God, and reverence for life.

Karma Yoga: the way of constructive, selfless action. The key to effective Karma Yoga practice is to fulfill personal duties without mental or emotional attachment to actions or their results.

Jnana (gyana) *Yoga*: the way of acquiring higher knowledge by cultivating powers of discriminative intelligence.

Raja Yoga: the way of contemplative meditation. The word *raja* indicates what is believed to be a superior, direct way to awaken to Self- and God-realization.

In some traditions, such as *Kriya Yoga*, the useful methods of all of the systems are practiced. *Kriyas* are "actions" performed (or that spontaneously occur) that remove mental and physical obstacles to Self- and God-realization.

An estimated 14 million people in the United States, and many more in Europe and other countries, now practice some form of Yoga. While the majority of them practice Hatha Yoga because of the physical and psychological benefits they experience, many integrate the practices of other yogic systems into their daily lifestyle routines.

yoga-sutras Sanskrit *sutra*, from the verb-root *siv*, to sew. Sutras are "threads" of concepts or teachings that describe a theory or explain what is intended to be communicated.

Patanjali (second century) compiled what was then known about yoga practices and presented it in a concise, systematic form. Superconscious states and the various means by which they can be realized, specific spiritual practices, their results, and stages of awakening to permanent liberation of consciousness are described.

Center for Spiritual Awareness

The international headquarters is located in the northeast Georgia mountains, ninety miles from Atlanta. Facilities include offices and publishing department, the main meeting hall and dining room, the Shrine of All Faiths Meditation Temple, two library buildings, six guest houses, and a bookstore.

Weekend and week long meditation retreats are offered on a donation basis from early spring until late autumn.

For a free information packet and book list, contact:

Center for Spiritual Awareness
Post Office Box 7
Lakemont, Georgia 30552-0001

Telephone 706-782-4723 weekdays 8 a.m. to 4 p.m.
Fax 706-782-4560
E-mail: csainc@csa-davis.org
Internet Web Site: www.csa-davis.org

Offices and retreat center on CSA Lane,
Lakemont (Rabun County), Georgia.

Give a copy of
Satisfying Our Innate Desire to Know God
to your spiritually inclined friends